HIGH-IMPACT
INTERVIEW
QUESTIONS

HIGH-IMPACT INTERVIEW QUESTIONS

SECOND EDITION

701 Behavior-Based Questions to
Find the Right Person for Every Job

VICTORIA A. HOEVEMEYER

Foreword by Paul Falcone

AMACOM

AMERICAN MANAGEMENT ASSOCIATION

New York • Atlanta • Brussels • Chicago • Mexico City • San Francisco
Shanghai • Tokyo • Toronto • Washington, D.C.

Bulk discounts available. For details, visit:
www.amacombooks.org/go/specialsales
Or contact special sales:
Phone: 800-250-5308
Email: specialsls@amanet.org
View all the AMACOM titles at: www.amacombooks.org
American Management Association: www.amanet.org

This publication is designed to provide accurate and authoritative information in regard to the subject matter covered. It is sold with the understanding that the publisher is not engaged in rendering legal, accounting, or other professional service. If legal advice or other expert assistance is required, the services of a competent professional person should be sought.

Library of Congress Cataloging-in-Publication Data

Names: Hoevemeyer, Victoria A., author.
Title: High-impact interview questions : 701 behavior-based questions to find
  the right person for every job / Victoria A. Hoevemeyer ; foreword by Paul
  Falcone.
Description: Second edition. | New York : American Management Association,
  [2017] | Includes bibliographical references and index.
Identifiers: LCCN 2017011156 (print) | LCCN 2017025874 (ebook) | ISBN
  9780814438831 (eBook) | ISBN 9780814438824 (pbk.)
Subjects: LCSH: Employment interviewing. | Psychology, Industrial.
Classification: LCC HF5549.5.I6 (ebook) | LCC HF5549.5.I6 H59 2017 (print) |
  DDC 658.3/1124--dc23
LC record available at https://lccn.loc.gov/2017011156

About AMA

American Management Association (www.amanet.org) is a world leader in talent development, advancing the skills of individuals to drive business success. Our mission is to support the goals of individuals and organizations through a complete range of products and services, including classroom and virtual seminars, webcasts, webinars, podcasts, conferences, corporate and government solutions, business books, and research. AMA's approach to improving performance combines experiential learning—learning through doing—with opportunities for ongoing professional growth at every step of one's career journey.

Printing number

10 9 8 7 6 5 4 3 2 1

To my father, Kurt, for all his love and support and in memory of
the two most incredible women I've ever known—
my grandmother, Dorothy Caroline Hiser,
and my mother, Donna Joyce.

CONTENTS

Foreword

THE CONCEPT OF behavior-based interviewing has been around for some time now, but nowhere is the art and technique developed as well as in Victoria Hoevemeyer's *High-Impact Interview Questions: 701 Behavior-Based Questions to Find the Right Person for Every Job*. Finally an entire text is dedicated to the critical task of framing interviewing questions around candidates' real-life experiences—questions that will prompt factual answers and focus on future competencies and abilities.

Interviewing has never been a simple process, primarily because we all know how hard people can be to read. Many job candidates are well-studied interviewees, but their performance, once hired, may not coincide with the superstar/hero figure they portrayed during initial evaluation. So much rides on hiring the right people—team camaraderie, group productivity, and a positive work environment—that one poor decision could set you and your team back significantly. It's not even uncommon to see managers who tend to leave positions unfilled for long periods of time for fear of hiring someone who doesn't fit in.

Fair enough, but we can't lead our business lives by avoidance or fear of making mistakes. If it's true that the productivity of human capital is the only profit lever in today's knowledge-based economy, then we've got to hire the best and brightest and develop them to their fullest potential. Your front-end "people reading" skills and selection abilities, therefore, will remain one of your most important portable skill sets as you advance in your own career.

Even if you're not totally comfortable now with your abilities in this area, fear not! Interviewing to make "high probability" hires (remember, no one's asking for "guarantees" when it comes to people forecasting) is a learnable skill. With just a little focus and commitment on your part, you can develop an interviewing routine that's uniquely yours. And employing a behavior-based interviewing format based on the competencies you value and hold dear will give you greater confidence in your abilities to spot talent, which in turn will result in stronger hires (which further strengthens your confidence!).

Behavioral interviewing is based on real analysis of historical on-the-job performance. Victoria Hoevemeyer's new book makes it so much easier to get to know the real candidate by providing you with competency-based questions for specific scenarios. Whether you're looking to identify corporate-wide competencies or job-specific competencies in a prospective new hire, you'll find behavioral questions specific to multiple scenarios.

The premise is simple: Behavioral interview techniques attempt to relate a candidate's answers to specific past experiences and focus on projecting potential performance from past actions. By relating a candidate's answers to specific past experiences, you'll develop a reliable indicator of how that individual will most likely perform in the future. Behavioral interview questioning strategies do not deny that people can learn from their mistakes and alter their behaviors. However, they do assume that future behavior will closely reflect past actions.

Furthermore, behavior-based questioning techniques ensure spontaneity since candidates can't prepare for them in advance. Rehearsed answers to traditional interview questions go by the wayside in an ad hoc environment where candidates tell stories about their real-life work performance. And because behavioral interview questions tie responses to concrete past events, candidates naturally minimize any inclination to exaggerate answers. Hence, you're assured of more accurate responses during your interview, and you're provided with specific information to use a little later down the line when checking references.

The unpredictable course of a behavior-based interview exchange may sound something like this:

You: Tell me what you like least about being a manager at your current company.

Candidate: Oh, it's definitely having to discipline, lay off, or terminate employees for poor performance. We've had a lot of restructuring in the past year or so.

You: Sure, that's understandable. I agree that's no fun. Tell me about the last time that you had to terminate someone for cause: What were the circumstances, and how did you handle it?

Candidate: Well, the most recent term for cause in my group happened about four months ago when a member of my staff just couldn't or wouldn't focus on his job. He made continuous errors on the manufacturing line, and it seemed like no amount of training or supervision could get him to focus on his work and lessen the breakage and scrap rate he was experiencing.

You: Oh, that's too bad. Tell me more about it.

Candidate: Well, I first went to the union steward and gave her a tip that he was having continuous problems because I knew that they were friends and that he trusted her. I thought she might be able to help him and quietly find out what was really bothering him. I also asked her to give him the Employee Assistance Program (EAP) brochure to make sure he had resources available to help him if personal issues in his life were getting in the way. Unfortunately, she came back to me a few days later, and said he "wouldn't let her in." Then she reminded me that since she was a union steward, she really couldn't be involved any further in any activities that could have negative ramifications for a union member, which I fully understood.

You: Interesting. What was your next step?

Candidate: Well, I then decided to go straight to the employee with his prior year's performance appraisal in hand. He had scored 4 out of 5, meaning that he had really done well, and I told him that I couldn't give him a 4 if I had to grade him right now. I honestly told him that if the performance evaluation period were right then and there, he'd probably get a score of 2, meaning that he didn't meet company expectations. I told him the good news, though, was that it wasn't the time for the annual evaluation and that it wasn't too late to turn things around. I just wanted to know if and how I could help. Unfortunately, he wouldn't open up to me either, so we just left it at that.

You: Did he realize he was heading down a path of termination?

Candidate: He certainly did. In fact, I ended that meeting letting him know that my door was always open if he needed anything, but that if there were any more problems with excessive breakage and scrap rate, I'd have no choice but to go to human resources and look into writing him up for substandard job performance. He even seemed apathetic when I said that.

You: So it sounds like you were very fair and open with him. *What is it about you* that made you want to speak with the union steward and employee first before going to human resources to initiate disciplinary action?

And so the story goes. What's important in this exercise is to see how comfortable and fluid the interview was. It was more of a discussion and "getting to know you" meeting rather than a formal, structured Q&A session with rote responses to one-dimensional questions. The key to a good interviewing style sometimes lies in making candidates feel comfortable enough to admit, "Well, I really wouldn't typically say this in an interview, but since I'm so comfortable with you, and since you're asking, I'll tell you . . . ." If you can establish rapport quickly and really help the candidate feel like she can put her guard down because you're trying to decide *together* if this opportunity is a right fit, then your interviewing skills will leapfrog past your competition. You'll also develop a reputation as a caring and concerned leader. After all, the leadership factor should always come into play during the very first interview.

In addition, it's always healthy to add self-appraisal questions to your behavior-based questioning techniques, which will add an honest and somewhat critical dimension to the candidate's responses. You can do that by simply using probing or follow-up questions. So your conversation might continue with additional queries like these:

"How would you handle it differently if you could do it all over again?"

"Could you argue that you either "jumped the gun" or waited too long to initiate progressive disciplinary action?"

"How would your boss grade you on how you handled this deteriorating performance situation in terms of your willingness to confront the problem head on?"

"In retrospect, was going to the union first a mistake? What kinds of downsides could it have caused?"

"What did the union say about your supervision in the grievance process, and what were its arguments to either avoid termination or to reinstate its member?"

"What is it about you that prompted you to handle this situation as you did?"

The insights gleaned from this behavior-based interviewing exchange are enormous. The "feel" you now have for this candidate after such a short exchange provides real insights into her approach toward supervision and leadership. What do you now know?

First, she's an open and honest communicator: Her going to the union steward in an effort to provide the employee with support from a trusted friend shows that she's a caring individual who places importance on interpersonal relationships. That being said, any time a manager approaches the union first before going to human resources may be a red flag in terms of where the manager's loyalties lie. If her going to the union is an exception based on a known personal relationship between the employee and that particular union steward, then the manager's decision may be understandable. Barring that personal friendship between the employee and the union steward, however, this could be seen as a real area of concern for your company.

Second, the candidate has solid follow-through skills and patience in allowing the union steward a few days' time to resolve the problem.

Third, this interviewee approached her employee in a positive manner—with last year's solid performance review in hand, attempting to motivate the worker by inspiring him to return to a higher performance level.

Fourth, she verbally forewarned the employee that failure to provide immediate and sustained improvement could result in further disciplinary action.

Fifth, when she went to human resources as a last resort, the worker surely wasn't surprised. The interviewee's ultimate decision to work with HR to terminate this individual for substandard job performance demonstrates that she confronts problems head-on, follows protocol, and stands behind her convictions. That's a pretty revealing role-play and a great use of your time during the interviewing process!

What also comes into initial play is a focus on the competencies that make someone successful in your organization. In this example, the candidate clearly demonstrates communication and listening skills, human concern, a willingness to confront problems head-on and in the spirit of mutual resolution, and the conviction to take punitive action if an employee refuses to rehabilitate himself despite the company's best efforts.

However, although this individual's overall responses may seem positive to you, others may find these same responses unacceptable. For example, some managers believe that going to the union for help—under *any* circumstances—is a mistake because unions represent, by definition, opposition. Along the same vein, some managers may feel that a union's presence and effectiveness should be minimized whenever possible so that the company's management team retains as much power and discretion in managing its employees as possible. Still others may feel that managers should always go to human resources first whenever a formal problem arises with a direct report.

Whatever the case, there will always be more room for differing interpretation when candidates respond to interview questions in a behavior-based, "story-telling" fashion. Simply stated, behavior-based questioning techniques provide much more *critical mass* to every interview so that the interviewer has a more thorough understanding of variances and nuances that could make a big difference in the ultimate decision to hire.

Hoevemeyer's book is structured around hundreds of similar examples using a technique called competency-based behavioral interviewing, or CBBI. The essence of CBBI is to ensure that a candidate possesses the skills, knowledge, and abilities to be successful in your group. CBBI accomplishes this by amplifying those job-related competencies that are mission critical and unique to your department's success.

More important, you'll find a lot of flexibility in this book in terms of honing in on those competencies, whether by technical performance area or by interpersonal communication ability. So whether you're focused on listening skills or building relationships, writing skills or political savvy, you'll have a host of behavior-based questions at your fingertips, replete with promptings for success stories and failure incidents.

This competency-based interviewing model is about *real* analysis of historical on-the-job performance. As such, it will set the tone and expectation for integration into other leadership practices as well. The very same competencies that you identify during initial candidate evaluation will dovetail nicely into your performance appraisal, training and development, and compensation and reward systems. And that's the goal—to identify key performers, integrate them smoothly onto your team, set their expectations in terms of what's valued and what will be evaluated, and then help them thrive.

Just remember that it all begins with a consistent, practical interview-questioning paradigm that will save you time, strengthen your candidate evaluation skills, and serve as a successful entrée into your organization's performance management system. Now at your fingertips you have a guiding hand and handy guide to get you there. Enjoy the book, and appreciate the potential that you have to lead, challenge, and motivate those around you.

—Paul Falcone

Author, *96 Great Interview Questions to Ask Before You Hire*

Acknowledgments

My continued appreciation for the help the following people provided in terms of technical assistance and feedback on the first edition: Steve and Lori Hoevemeyer, Joe Giglio, and Debbie McQuaide.

As with the first edition, continued thanks goes to William Miller for his patience, support, and encouragement as he listened to me talk about and brainstorm parts of the second edition for months and months.

Special second edition thanks goes to Debbie Dover for reviewing some of the material and for sharing her insights and perspectives.

Finally, and most importantly, I'd like to thank my parents, Kurt and Donna, for their support and encouragement through all my endeavors in life—those they understood, as well as those they didn't.

INTRODUCTION

When I facilitate interview skills learning programs, I always ask how many of the hiring managers in attendance enjoy interviewing and how many of them feel that it's a value-added component of their job. For the most part, a very small percentage of leaders raise their hand for either question.

One of the reasons that hiring managers dislike interviewing is that they feel so overworked and overwhelmed that the thought of having to go through the interviewing and selection process depresses them. They feel that it's an imposition that is just going to make it even harder for them to get their jobs done. As a result, they end up rushing through the process and focusing more on hiring a "warm body" than a great-fit candidate. This often ends up as a vicious cycle when the "warm body" needs to be terminated for performance or behavioral issues and the interview process has to begin again. That longer-term focus, though, is often hard to grasp when the hiring manager constantly feels "behind the eight ball." A great example of this is one hiring manager I followed up with because he hadn't been responding to a recruiter. He explained his lack of response this way: "I have ten projects I'm working on right now. Literally. I can show you the list. And they all have short deadlines. I can review these résumés and set up interviews to fill the position and miss deadlines that may cost me my job, or I can get the projects done and live to work another day. As a team, we can survive for a while without the position being filled. I can't continue to survive without my job."

Those who don't enjoy interviewing often fall back on the fact that they were never taught to interview. When you don't feel you know what you're doing—and you add a few bad hires on top of that—it's almost guaranteed to create an avoidance reaction to interviewing. The process then becomes as painful for the interviewer as it is for the candidate.

Just as dangerous are those hiring managers who say they enjoy doing it, but (knowingly or unknowingly) do it very poorly. I had one hiring manager who proudly said that interviewing was easy. He went on to explain that for every job, he had a one-question interview guide. The singular question was "Why should I hire you?" He explained that everything you needed to know about the candidate was contained in their answer to that question. If you ask them a few follow-up questions, he contended, you can figure out the best candidate for any position in less than half an hour. By the way, this was a human resources leader!

I wish I had the magic bullet to help hiring managers understand that the recruitment and selection process is one of the most important tasks they will undertake. When, as a hiring manager, you take the time to select the right people, you make your job as a leader significantly easier. However, when you hire the wrong person, you've made your already overfilled schedule even worse.

A bad hiring decision will not only affect you directly, but may also have repercussions throughout the entire organization. At the very least, a bad hiring decision has the potential of:

- **Having a negative impact on your bottom line.** Hiring mistakes that result in terminations and having to refill the position are costly. This can range from 5 percent of base salary for an hourly position up to 100 (or more) times base salary for senior level positions. And that doesn't account for the time and money you spend trying to salvage that bad hire.
- **Negatively impacting your day-to-day operations.** If you—or a member of your team—are having to spend extra time coaching or training an employee who "just doesn't get it," that means that something else (usually something important) isn't getting done.
- **Playing a critical role in determining the team's ability to achieve its annual goals and objectives.** If your staff are trying

to train or cover for a new employee who isn't cutting it, that impacts their ability to successfully do their jobs. If this new person interacts with customers—and does so poorly—there is the potential for customer loss or, at the very least, significant service recovery efforts.

- **Loss of key players on your team.** If you are constantly asking your team members—particularly the high-performing team members—to help train a new employee who is continuing to have performance issues, it may get to the point that the high-performing employee chooses to go elsewhere so as not to have to deal with this problem. Great employees want to work with other great employees. If you don't provide that environment, the best will likely go elsewhere.
- **Negatively impact morale.** It's really difficult for employees to stay positive when there is a "problem" employee, who is probably getting paid a salary comparable to theirs, that they constantly have to help or cover for.
- **Creating havoc with other tactical and strategic directives.**

I wish I could say that this book will take the pain out of interviewing or that it will result in a great hire every time. Unfortunately, I can't say either of those. What I can say is that this book will provide some anesthesia to the pain of the interviewing process. The anesthesia comes in the form of competency-based behavioral interviewing (CBBI)—which is not anywhere nearly as cumbersome, intimidating, or complicated as it may sound.

CBBI is simply a structured interview process that focuses on gathering specific, job-related, real-world examples of behaviors the candidate has demonstrated on previous jobs. Because of its focus on competencies, CBBI minimizes the impact of personal impressions and biases that can occur during the interview, which result in subjective hiring decisions. CBBI is intended to help you determine if the candidate is a match for the technical, special, and functional skills required for the position and, most importantly, ensure that the candidate possesses the competencies for success in the position and is a fit with the team and the organization.

While this book examines a variety of issues relative to the recruitment process (e.g., culture fit, legal and illegal interview questions, making the hiring decision), the focus is on the CBBI questions themselves. This is because one of the primary reasons people cite for not using CBBI is the difficulty in coming up with good, relevant, appropriate questions. This book takes the time, confusion, and complication out of the equation. Once the competencies for the position are determined, it is simply a matter of turning to the list of sample questions for that competency and selecting the question(s) that best solicit the type of information you need to determine whether or not the candidate is a good fit.

So if you are looking for new or better ways to assess the likelihood that the candidates will produce the kind of on-the-job performance needed for success, to reduce the percentage of "bad hires," or simply to enhance your current competency- or behavior-based interviewing process, you've come to the right place.

INTERVIEWING: THE WAY IT IS (WARTS AND ALL)

BEHAVIOR-BASED INTERVIEWING, OR competency-based interviewing, has been used in some organizations for around forty years. Many organizations, however, continue to use a traditional interview format, which is sometimes interlaced with situational (also called scenario, hypothetical, or "what if") interview questions. The newest kid on the block is the brain twister interview question.

Before getting into competency- or behavior-based interviewing, let's start by taking a look at each of the other interviewing techniques.

Traditional Interview Questions

Almost everyone is familiar with traditional interview questions. This would include questions such as:

- Why should I hire you?
- What are your greatest strengths/weaknesses?
- What did you enjoy most/least about your last position?
- Where do you want to be in five years?
- Why should I hire you?
- How well do you work under pressure/stress/tight deadlines?
- Describe the best boss you've ever had.
- Walk me through your work history.

From an interviewer's standpoint, far too many of us can, in our sleep, ask these types of questions. And we are so familiar with the answers that we can almost recite them word-for-word with the candidate.

There are not many candidates who have interviewed for a position who have not been asked most—if not all—of these questions. While there are some candidates who find comfort in these types of questions because they have pat answers for them, many are frustrated because they feel that their true strengths and potential contributions are not coming through.

Traditional Questions' "Unique" Offspring

I would be remiss if I failed to talk about a variation of the traditional interview question. It is a subcategory of questions that I kindly refer to as "unique." This includes questions such as:

- Who are your heroes and what makes them your heroes?
- If you found a penguin in your freezer, what would you do?
- What is the funniest thing that's happened to you recently?
- If you were a bicycle, what part would you be?
- What is your favorite color and what does it reflect in your personality?
- If you were on a merry-go-round, what song would you be singing?
- If your life had a theme song, what would it be?

There are hiring managers who extol the virtue of questions like these. They swear that the candidate's answers will provide significant insights. By asking such questions, proponents say, they will find out how creative a person is, gain an understanding of the candidate's ability to think on his feet, be able to measure his ability to deal with ambiguity, and determine whether he is able to . . . well, you get the idea.

Advantages of Traditional Interviews

One of the most significant advantages of the traditional interview format is that people understand it and are comfortable with it. While many candidates are nervous going into an interview, the traditional format—since it is a known interviewing approach—will often put them at ease a little faster than other types of interviews.

Second, in most situations, traditional interviews allow for a significant number of questions to be asked in a relatively short period of time. Many traditional interview questions require short answers (e.g., "What are your strengths?"). Even for those questions that require a longer answer, the answer tends not to exceed thirty seconds.

Finally, some traditional questions may reveal fit or non-fit with the position (e.g., "What would your ideal job look like?"), the position's manager (e.g., "What are you looking for in a boss?"), or the organization's culture (e.g., "What kind of organization would you like to work for?").

The only advantage in sprinkling your interview with "unique" interview questions is that they may help you gauge whether the candidate is able to keep a straight face when confronted with something completely unexpected and whether (but not the extent to which) she can think on her feet.

The problem with "unique" questions is they have nothing even remotely to do with the candidate's ability to do the job. They are simply silly, time-wasting questions. Any insight an interviewer gains from asking such questions is purely conjecture and supposition. There is no research to indicate that there is any predictive value in these questions.

Further, by asking such "unique" questions, you may just put off a strong, highly qualified candidate. There is a relatively large pool of candidates who question whether they really want to work for a company that uses a person's favorite color as the basis of any part of a hiring decision.

These are not, by the way, obscure questions I made up. Each and every one of the questions listed above really have been asked of candidates during an interview.

What's the Problem with Traditional Interviews?

The major problem with traditional interview questions is that virtually every one of them has become a cliché. There are thousands of books and websites that provide candidates with the "right" answer to the "top 100 interview questions." The really creative candidates will also purchase the books and go to the websites designed for recruiters and hiring managers. These resources provide them with what to look for when the candidate answers question X. This information, then, enables them to fine-tune their perfect answers to each of your questions.

Ask most hiring managers which candidate truly stood out in a series of interviews for a particular position, and you are likely to get a blank stare. The primary reason is that it's hard to distinguish one candidate from another, other than through the eloquence of their presentation. Almost every candidate has memorized—in their own words—the "right" answer to all the questions. As a result, what sends one person to the top of the candidate pile is less likely to be his fit with the competencies required for success in the position and more likely to be the hiring manager's gut feeling that the person will be successful.

Situational Interview Questions

The second type of question you will find in interviews is situational questions, also referred to as scenario-based interviewing, hypothetical questions, or "what-if" questions. In a situational interview, candidates are asked how they would handle a particular situation. In some cases, this is built around a specific scenario (see the third through sixth bullet points below). Questions that fall into this category might include:

- What would you do if someone higher than you in the organization instructed you to do something that was unethical or illegal?
- How would you handle a situation where you had conflicting information with which to make a decision?
- Your boss has to leave town to handle an urgent customer problem. He has handed off a project to you that needs to be done for the company's president prior to his return. Initially, you feel your boss has done a good job of briefing you on the project, but

as you get into it, you have more questions than answers. You aren't able to reach your boss, and you are running out of time. What would you do?

- A customer brings in a product for repair on Monday, is told that it is a simple repair, and that it would be ready by 3 P.M. on Tuesday. When the customer comes in at 4 P.M. on Tuesday, the product has still not been repaired. The customer is very unhappy. As the service manager, how would you handle the situation?
- You and a coworker are jointly working on a project, having divided up work in a manner you both agreed to. Your coworker has not been doing the work she agreed to do. What would you do?
- You are a member of a cross-functional team dealing with a difficult problem. The team members have diverse views and sometimes hold very strong opinions or positions. You are constantly in conflict with one of the other team members. How would you establish a satisfactory working relationship with this person to accomplish the team's goals?

The advantage of a situational interview is that, in most situations, it is relatively easy to match the candidate's answer to the required answer for the position. For example, if you are looking for a specific six-step process for handling difficult customers, you can check off the steps the candidate lists against the steps used in the organization. This, then, makes it relatively easy to evaluate and rate the answer. You get different information for the candidate who only hits on two of the six steps than for the candidate who got all six steps but got two of them mixed up in order, or the candidate who lists and explains all six steps in the exact order you have listed.

If you are interviewing entry-level people who may have limited experience, but who have a wide knowledge base, these types of questions may be appropriate. They will tell you that the candidate knows, intellectually, the process that should be used to address certain situations.

The Problem with Situational/Hypothetical Questions

The primary problem with hypothetical questions is that they assume that people actually do as they say they will do (or act as they say they will act). This, as we know, doesn't always happen. For example, I have been facilitating skill-based conflict management programs for about 25 years. I could walk a trained monkey (and maybe even an untrained one) through the steps. How often do you think I use that process when, after asking three times, I still don't have the information that I asked for in a report? Let me give you a hint: not consistently!

For many of us, there is, unfortunately, a weak correlation between knowing the right thing to do or the right process to follow and actually doing the right thing under pressure, while distracted, when in a time crunch, or even sometimes when everything is calm.

Some hiring managers feel that they are able to get around this disconnect by asking a follow-up question like, "Give me an example of when you used this skill or process." And then guess what happens? Almost 100 percent of the time, the candidates' examples will match, letter-for-letter, word-for-word, the exact process or skill steps they just described. Does that mean that they practice what they preach? Maybe. But maybe it just means that they are good at putting the "right" process or skill steps into a nice illustrative story and tying it up with a pretty bow for you.

Brainteaser Interview Questions

The third category of questions was pioneered by Microsoft and has been used by many of the high-tech companies for a number of years. Interestingly, some companies, including Google, are starting to give up on these types of questions. According to Laszlo Bock, former senior vice president of people operations at Google, in his book *Work Rules!*, brainteaser questions are "... at best a discrete skill that can be improved by practice. ... At worst, they rely on some trivial bit of information or insight that is withheld from the candidate, and serve primarily to make the interviewer feel clever or self-satisfied. They have little if any ability to predict how candidates will perform in a job."

Unfortunately, these questions have not disappeared from the interview process in all organizations. As recently as 2016, candidates report, on Glassdoor.com, being asked brainteaser questions—and many of these candidates report being mystified as to why the questions were asked. Some questions that fall into this category include:

- If you could remove any one of the fifty U.S. states, which would it be and why?
- A man is lying dead in the middle of a forest, in the middle of a puddle, in a scuba suit. How did he die?
- You have a three-gallon jug and a five-gallon jug. How would you measure out exactly four gallons?
- How would you weigh an airplane without using a scale?

Proponents of the brainteaser interview questions allege that they enable the interviewer to uncover qualities about a candidate that can't be discovered from the résumé or other interviewing techniques. Further, they believe that these types of questions will provide information on:

- How well the person performs under stress
- The processes the candidate uses to analyze a problem
- The candidate's critical thinking skills
- How creative or innovative a solution the candidate can come up with
- How intelligent the person is
- How the candidate thinks, especially when faced with an unexpected issue
- How the person reacts to unanticipated challenges or difficult problems

What are the advantages of brainteaser interviews? A hiring manager might want to consider asking a brainteaser question when interviewing a relatively new graduate for a highly technical position. This may give the candidate an opportunity to demonstrate his analytical thinking skills when practical experience is not available.

Another potential advantage of a brainteaser question (not an interview based on them, though) would be the opportunity to gauge a candidate's reaction to the playfulness and innovation that can be inherent in these questions (assuming, that is, that she enjoys that kind of mental gymnastics). It would also give the interviewer an opportunity to eavesdrop on the candidate's thinking processes.

The Problem with Brainteaser Questions

There is no problem if you listen to and believe people like William Poundstone, author of *How Would You Move Mount Fuji?*, who says, "If you don't judge people on the basis of something like these puzzles, you're probably going to be judging them on the basis of how firm their handshake is or whether you like how they're dressed, which are even less relevant." However, as quoted in Thad Peterson's Monster.com article, "Brainteaser or Interview Torture Tool?," Poundstone also points out that "while various industries have glommed onto this interviewing trend, it makes little sense for many types of workers."

According to proponents, brainteaser questions will tell you how the person thinks and how smart they are: they will highlight their rational and logical thinking, planning, problem-solving, and decision-making skills and facilities. They will also, some pundits say, show you how people process information.

Proponents say that these types of questions will lead to creative and original answers that haven't been rehearsed by the candidate. While this may be the case at this point, there will come a time—most likely sooner than later—when this will not be true. There are an increasing number of books and Internet sites that provide the "right" answer (or the preferred thought process) for answering many of these questions. It is possible that, in a short period of time, there will be a plethora of candidates interviewing at companies known for using this technique who already know the answers to the questions.

This could lead to an interesting situation. Imagine this situation:

You ask a candidate a brainteaser question during an interview. Unbeknownst to you, the candidate knows the "right" answer to the question. Because she wants the job, and because she knows she can "fake" thinking through the question out loud, she chooses to play the game and answer the question.

Since you will never know whether the candidate already knew the answer to the question or whether she was smart enough to figure out the "right" answer, does it cause you to wonder about the value of these types of questions?

I won't argue against the point that it is important to understand where a candidate's skill level is and, when appropriate, to know their level of creativity. However, what I have not been able to figure out for the life of me is how someone's answer to "How many piano tuners are there in Chicago?" is going to enable you to determine a candidate's fit with the requirements for the position. You can, of course, make suppositions and assumptions, but do you really want to hire someone that way?

The ability to solve the brainteaser (to get the "right" answer or to answer to the interviewer's satisfaction) may indicate a level of ingenuity, cunning, and even mental dexterity. Whether those are indicators of a candidate's ability to successfully demonstrate the competencies of the position is uncertain. If ingenuity is a competency, the answer may well be yes; if, however, the competency is problem solving, maybe not. For most positions, a candidate's ability to solve a brainteaser is not a valid and predictive factor for their successful performance of the position's competencies.

Stepping Back to the Big Picture

The bottom line is that a big part of the reason these three types of questions continue to dominate organizations is that most managers, when they are asked, are not shy about telling you what good interviewers they are. They say that they have a good "intuitive read" on the answers that candidates provide; they "know in their gut" when someone is "being straight with them." I even had one executive in a service organization tell me (with a straight face) that all she needed to do was look at what the person was doing in the lobby to be able to tell if they were going to work out or not.

Many hiring managers will swear that they get incredible insights into a person when they know things like what the candidate does in her free time and what books she has recently read. (Yes, I have had hiring managers go on and on about all they have learned from candidates' answers to these questions.)

Some hiring managers have gone so far as to tell me that they have virtually infallible instincts. One manager told me that he could "smell a bad candidate a mile away," even though his department had a 25 percent turnover rate in an industry that typically had, at the time, about a 10 percent turnover rate.

Unfortunately, hiring on gut reactions, infallible instinct, or a single traditional interview question rarely leads to good hires. More often than not, it results in the hiring manager employing someone just like himself or someone who interviews well rather than someone whose skills and experiences are a best fit for the position and the organization.

The bottom line is that there is really only one problem with traditional, situational, and brainteaser interview questions: They fail to focus on the demonstrable behavior that will provide sufficient information upon which to determine whether the candidates can do the job for which they are being interviewed.

Before we proceed to the next chapter, it's important to clarify one thing: I'm not saying that you absolutely, positively have to get rid of all of these types of questions in order to have an acceptable interviewing and hiring process. (After all, doing anything cold turkey is tough.) What I am recommending is that, if you must use some of them, do three things: First, make them a small percentage of the questions you ask rather than the basis of the interview. Second, ask the same questions of every candidate. And third, make the basis of your interview one that is more effective, more predictive, and (if done properly) more legally defensible: competency-based behavioral interviewing.

COMPETENCY-BASED BEHAVIORAL INTERVIEWING (CBBI): THE WHAT, WHEN, AND WHY

THE PRIMARY REASON a company conducts an interview is to learn enough about a candidate to determine whether the person will be successful on the job. There are three parts to this success:

1. Having the technical skills and knowledge
2. Having the functional skills and abilities
3. Being able to demonstrate the position's competencies

The vast majority of interviews focus on the first two components for success; many fail to consider competency proficiency.

When Gillian, the regional manager, interviewed Peter for store manager for a nationwide retail chain store, she was convinced that fortune was on her side. Peter had extensive budget experience—beyond what was required for the position. He had done scheduling for a number of years and successfully dealt with the challenges of staffing around the holidays. In his last job, he used the same payroll processing company. His business and financial knowledge was thorough—and exemplary. The few minor issues that she uncovered were things that would be addressed as part of the company's New Store Manager Training process. The only reason Peter was looking for a new job was that he was tired of the commute to his current employer, which was one hour each way.

At this point, some of you may be thinking, "Anything that sounds too good to be true is probably too good to be true." And you would be right. It took Gillian about a month to go from elated to concerned—and another month for her to become completely frustrated.

Peter had completed the New Store Manager Training program and been in the store for about a month when Gillian started getting calls, emails, and letters from customers complaining about Peter. They complained that he was rude, sarcastic, and condescending. Two long-time clerks left within a month of Peter taking over the store, saying in their exit interviews that they were leaving for more money. Other clerks started leaving shortly after that, making the store's turnover rate twice what it was at other stores.

Gillian sent in a secret shopper whom she had used before and who knew the store and employees fairly well. The secret shopper reported back that morale was through the floor and that when she walked out of the store, she was almost as depressed as the employees.

So what went wrong? As often happens in organizations, Gillian hired a person who was technically and functionally perfect for the position. Unfortunately, Peter was not interviewed against the competencies for success in the position, which included *managing conflict, maintaining a high customer focus*, and *building high-performance teams.* Had he been interviewed for these competencies, he probably would not have been hired.

In the vast majority of positions, the single factor that will distinguish one employee from another is the ability to exhibit the competencies for the position. When you identify and define competencies, and then interview against them—*in addition to* considering the technical and functional aspects—you are increasing the likelihood that the candidate you hire is the one who will truly be most successful.

What Is Competency-Based Behavioral Interviewing?

Before we define competency-based behavioral interviewing (CBBI), it's important that we define a competency. Simply put, a *competency* is a behavior (a skill and/or ability) or set of behaviors that describes the expected performance in a particular work context. The context could be for an organization, a functional job group (e.g., accounting, human resources, operations), a job category (e.g., senior managers, middle managers, professionals), or a specific job. When they are appropriately developed, competencies are the standards of success for the position and the behaviors that are needed to support the strategic plan, vision, mission, and goals of the organization.

Competencies are different from the other requirements one might find for a given position, such as technical skills, functional skills and knowledge, education, and experience. For example, it is one thing to recruit for a position and require five years of management experience. It is another thing to recruit for a position that requires five years of management experience leading a diverse group of people. In the second situation, you would be looking for a candidate with five years of management experience coupled with a demonstrated competency of *valuing diversity.*

Competency-based behavioral interviewing is a structured interview process that combines competencies with the premise that, with few exceptions:

- The best predictor of future performance/behavior is past performance/behavior.
- The more recent the performance/behavior, the more likely it is to be repeated.

The questions asked during CBBI are based on real situations that relate to the competencies for the position. Candidates, then, are evaluated based on actual behaviors/performance rather than on possible or potential behaviors/performance. As a result, the information gathered from candidates is significantly more predictive of what their behavior and performance are likely to be in the position for which they are interviewing than what one finds with other interviewing styles.

In CBBI, rather than asking candidates directly if they have a particular competency—to which you will almost always hear a resounding "yes!"—the interviewer asks the candidate to provide an example of a time when he demonstrated the competency. The focus is on the candidate giving you an indication of her proficiency in a particular competency by relating a real-world experience.

Typical interviews will sound something like this:

Interviewer: I think I mentioned earlier that this is a high-stress position. How do you manage stress?

Candidate: My last two positions were high stress. I actually do some of my best work under stress. Through experience, I've learned how to make stress work for me rather than against me. I think two of the most effective stress management techniques are . . .

Based on the answer the candidate provided, what do you really know about this person's ability to handle stress? Not much—other than the person knows a couple stress management techniques. Whether the person actually uses them or not is up for debate.

What is stressful to this candidate? Your guess is as good as mine. It could be that having to work the rest of the day after getting a paper cut is high stress for this candidate.

Using CBBI techniques, the interviewer would, instead, say something like this:

Interviewer: Tell me about a time you had to perform a task or project under a lot of stress.

Now you are going to find out how the candidate actually handled stress in a real-life situation and what she considers stressful. When used in conjunction with probing/follow-up questions, this question is going to provide significantly more information for comparing candidates to the competency requirements of the position and the culture of the organization than the answer you would receive to the original question. This ensures that the candidate will relate a real-life story rather than a hypothetical one.

How Is CBBI Different from Other Interviewing Styles?

When done properly, CBBI is different from the three interview styles discussed in Chapter 1 in at least seven ways.

1. CBBI is designed through a process—beginning with a job, function, and/or organizational analysis—to determine the competencies. Every question asked during a CBBI, then, can be traced back to the initial analysis. The purpose of every question and its contribution to the interview process—and the position—can be clearly and concisely explained. Because of this linked approach, interviewers do not ask irrelevant questions or any question that will not provide specific job-related, competency-based information.

2. Interview questions are planned and directly tied to the competencies for success in the position. A CBBI has specific questions that each interviewer will ask of each and every candidate for the position. This does not mean that there is no flexibility to delve into the candidate's experiences in more detail or get further clarification on something the candidate has said or insinuated. It simply means that every candidate is asked the same initial questions. Follow-up or probing questions will most likely vary from candidate to candidate.

3. Interviewers are trained on the CBBI process. When interviewers receive the training and guidance they need to be good, thorough interviewers, their confidence goes up, their ability to listen well increases, and they are more likely to reach an objective decision.

4. Rating scales are provided to minimize the subjectivity of the interviewing process. When the levels of proficiency for a competency are clearly defined, there tends to be less debate (or argument) between interviewers in terms of the rating a candidate should receive on a given competency.

5. Interview questions focus on actual current and past behavior rather than "might do" behavior. In most interview situations,

a candidate may say, "Were I faced with X situation, I would follow Y process." Unfortunately, you don't know whether the candidate, when called upon to use the process, will actually do what she says. With CBBI, the candidate is telling you exactly and specifically what she did—or didn't—do.

For example, imagine you were hiring a customer service representative. In a traditional interview, you might ask, "Have you had to deal with difficult customers in the past?" In a situational interview, you may pose a difficult customer situation and ask, "How would you handle that?" Using a CBBI process, you identified competencies for the position, one of which would (I would hope) be *customer focus*. One of the behavioral questions you would ask each candidate then might be, "Tell me about the most difficult customer you have ever had to deal with." The candidate's answer to this question will provide you with two valuable pieces of information that you would not get from the traditional or situational approach.

First, it will tell you what the candidate considers to be an extremely difficult customer. Imagine that *your* most difficult customers would typically make Attila the Hun look like a charmer. Now when you ask the candidate about his most difficult customer, he tells you a story about a customer who is about as difficult as you would expect the Queen of England ever to get (which is not very difficult). In this situation, then, there is probably not a good fit. It is highly unlikely that this person would be able to adequately and appropriately handle the intensity of customer reaction that may be experienced in the position for which he is applying.

Second, the candidate's answer will tell you how he has dealt with difficult customers in the past. In most situations— particularly if it is recent behavior the candidate is sharing— the behavior in the example will most likely be the behavior he will display when dealing with your difficult customers.

6. CBBI makes it easier to compare candidates because they are all measured against the same criteria. These criteria come

from the analysis that is conducted at the very beginning of the process. First, they are measured against criteria that can be found on the résumé. Those that pass that standard are then measured against the telephone screening interview criteria. Finally, those that pass that standard are then measured during the interview against the same competencies by answering the same questions.

7. CBBI focuses exclusively on competencies that are job-related. It doesn't presume to be able to intuit people's problem-solving ability (or any other ability) by their answer to a vague question. It does not assume that people who are technical and functionally qualified will necessarily be the best people for the position. CBBI takes a multidimensional approach to hiring. First, it uses technical and functional knowledge, skills, and abilities to narrow the candidate field. Then, it uses a focused telephone screening interview to identify the candidates who have the critical skills (non-résumé technical and functional expertise and, in many situations, baseline competencies). Finally, it uses an interviewing process that focuses on the competencies for success in the position to determine the best candidate for the position.

In short, CBBI allows you—the interviewer—the opportunity to gather factual, real-world evidence as to the candidate's ability to appropriately and effectively utilize the competencies required for success in the position and in the organization. As a result, you find out:

- Whether or not the candidate possesses the required competencies
- The candidate's skill level on that competency
- How the candidate is likely to demonstrate his/her skill level in that competency in the future

Moving to CBBI

While some work is involved in moving from a traditional, situational, or brainteaser format to a competency-based one, the good news is that the format will endure until the competencies for the position change. This means that if you conduct interviews on a quarterly basis for a particular position, you will be able to use the identical interview forms every time, until the competencies for the position change. Even if some of the competencies change, it is a matter of replacing that part of the interview process rather than starting over from scratch.

To make the move, you will need to go through a six-step process:

Step 1: Determine the Structure for the Competency Model(s)

The first step involves examining the optional competency model approaches and determining the optimal approach for your organization's culture and values. There are, basically, five different approaches an organization can take to establishing competencies.

Approach One: Organization-Wide. This approach would tie into the strategic direction of the organization and would apply to everyone in the organization. The question driving an organization-wide competency model would be: "What are the mission-critical competencies that everyone in this company needs to demonstrate if we are to achieve our strategic plan?" The answers to this question are used as the basis for developing the competency model.

The advantage of this approach is that every employee in the organization is united around a common set of competencies, even though the required level of proficiency may vary. The disadvantage is that, at times, the competencies become so generic and watered down that employees don't understand their importance or value to their day-to-day work lives.

Approach Two: Corporate Build. In this approach, there would be a set of competencies that apply to every individual in the organization. Then, as one goes up the levels in the organization, additional competencies are added. For example, a supervisor would have all of the organizational competencies, plus supervisor competencies; a manager would have all of the organizational competencies and supervisor competencies, plus managerial competencies, and so forth.

This is generally the least time-consuming approach to building an organizational competency model (other than just having a single set of competencies from top to bottom in an organization). It also ties all of the levels in the organization together through a set of common competencies. At times, however, it can result in far too many competencies once one gets to the top management level.

Approach Three: By Level. In this approach, each level in the organization would have a set of competencies unique to that level. The most commonly used division for this approach is:

- Hourly
- Office/Professional
- Supervisor
- Management
- Executive

While this approach is sometimes slightly more time-consuming than a Corporate Build, there are a couple of reasons that organizations elect to develop their competency model this way. First, it correlates very well with the succession planning methodology of preparing high potentials for any executive level position rather than for a specific position. Another advantage is that it can often result in a more manageable number of competencies more quickly than with a Corporate Build.

The biggest drawback to this approach for some organizations may be the lack of common core competencies throughout the organization. Because of this, some organizations elect to use a Modified Corporate Build approach, where there is a set of four to six organization-wide competencies and four to seven additional competencies specific to the organizational level.

Approach Four: By Function/Department. In this approach, there are competencies established for each function or department in the organization. Everyone in that function or department has the same competencies, regardless of their level or position in the organization. To reflect the fact that the extent of proficiency required for a given competency varies from one position to another, one can apply a weighting factor to each competency on the performance review form (e.g., the level of proficiency on a *continuous improvement* competency would be weighted higher for a manager than for an entry-level staff position).

Although the time involved in this approach, and the value it presents to the organization, varies significantly from organization to organization, some organizations find that what it takes to be successful in that organization can be more clearly defined by the function/department than it can be by level. The potential hazard faced in this approach is the tendency to become mired in the task and technical aspects of the function/department rather than focusing on the competencies necessary for success.

Approach Five: By Position. In this approach, competencies are established for each position in the organization. This is, by far, the most time-consuming approach to building a competency model. It is, however, also the most complete because it focuses specifically on the position. Organizations that use this approach believe that even at a given level in the organization, the competencies for success vary significantly from position to position. That is, for example, the competencies for a maintenance supervisor are significantly different from the competencies for a production supervisor. Further, the belief is that there are enough different competencies for a maintenance supervisor than a maintenance director to justify having a separate set of competencies for each.

There is no one "best" way to approach the development of competencies. The key to success is to ensure that the approach taken is one that fits with the organization's culture and values and one that supports the organization's strategic direction.

Step 2: Determine and Define the Competencies

One of the biggest advantages of following the CBBI process is that you define the competencies for success completely independently of the current employees or potential future candidates. Your focus is on the technical, functional, and special skills and on the competencies required for success.

Every organization has a different approach for determining competencies. The competencies listed in this book can be used as a starting point for developing individual competency models. There is also a wide range of tools available on the market that will provide guidance in determining the competencies. Regardless of the method or approach used, the competencies need to be clear success factors: competencies that are mission critical to the success of the individual and the organization.

How the competency is defined will also vary from organization to organization. The individual slant that an organization puts on the competency definition is what makes that generic competency unique to their organization. Let's look at some possible definitions for the competency *influencing*:

- Presents results-oriented ideas to peers and higher management; is able to build relationships that encourage others to support their ideas; makes and keeps commitments; cooperates with you.
- Is able to persuade others; builds consensus through give and take; gains cooperation from others to obtain information and accomplish goals; facilitates win-win situations.
- Uses appropriate interpersonal styles and methods to inspire and guide individuals and gain their acceptance of ideas and plans.

While the definitions are similar, each has a slightly different focus. This variation will have an impact on the rating scale used for the competency and on the interview questions asked. Regardless of how the company defines its competencies, the "acid test" will always be that, when asked, a random sample of employees will define a given competency in essentially the same manner.

One thing to consider in establishing competencies, regardless of the method, is focusing on the competencies that will drive the position and the company into the future. For example, imagine a company that has not, in many years, had to be particularly innovative—they have had an enduring product line. The company foresees, however, changes in the market that will require innovation at all levels. As a result, the company establishes a company-wide *creativity and innovation* competency.

For existing employees, the company begins offering developmental opportunities (special projects, classroom training programs, e-learning, reading materials, etc.), and begins recognizing and rewarding creative and innovative projects and ideas. For recruitment, a *creativity and innovation* competency is added to the CBBI process. As a result, the company begins to hire people who possess this competency. Now, the company has begun to build a culture of which *creativity and innovation* are a critical part.

Step 3: Determine the Interview Questions

Typically, this is the most arduous part of the process. Fortunately, you were wise enough to purchase this book, making this step relatively simple and straightforward. Simply turn to the page that lists your competency and, using your definition of that competency, select the questions you will ask to determine a candidate's proficiency at that competency.

Once you determine the questions, they will be used consistently until there is a need to change either a competency or a question within a competency. How these questions are divided up among the interviewers may, however, change. The two variables are the number of people who will be interviewing candidates and how many interviews candidates will need to go through before a hiring decision is made.

If, for example, you have ten competencies, and two questions under each competency, you would have twenty questions. If you have two people interviewing and you will be doing two rounds of interviews before making a selection, you would have each interviewer asking five questions during each interview round.

How do you determine which competencies and/or which questions each interviewer will ask? One approach would be to ask the questions associated with the mission-critical competencies during the first round of interviews and the questions associated with the remaining competencies during the second round of interviews. Another possible approach is to ask one question from each competency during the first round of interviews (five per interviewer) and the other question from each competency during the second round of interviews.

Step 4: Develop the Rating Scale(s)

To minimize the variation of ratings from one interviewer to another, interviewers can be provided with a rating scale against which to evaluate candidate responses. Chapter 7 explores rating scale options in detail.

Step 5: Design the Organization's Interview Formats

There are two formats that should be designed if the organization is going to maximize the CBBI process. The first is the telephone screening interview format. Chapter 6 provides an overview of the purpose of and the process for telephone screening interviews. The second format the organization will need to design is the face-to-face interview, which is discussed in Chapter 7.

Step 6: Provide Training to All Interviewers

Investing a little bit of money in training interviewers and hiring managers is probably the best investment you can make in your CBBI interviewing and selection process—and for the organization as a whole—to improve interviewer skills and reduce interviewer rating errors. The level and detail of the training will depend on how involved the people who will be interviewing are in the development of the interviewing tools. At minimum, the training should cover topics such as:

- How much time to spend on each part of the interview
- Developing a consistent message about the job
- Presenting a company-wide, consistent message about the organization
- How to use rating scales
- Asking questions and listening for STAR answers (STAR stands for Situation, Task, Action, Results; see Chapter 7 for more information on STAR.)
- How to use the telephone screening interview form
- How to use the face-to-face interview form

- Probing for additional information
- Legal and illegal queries
- Taking notes
- The process for discussing candidates and making a hiring decision

It is also important, as part of the training, for participants (interviewers and hiring managers) to have an opportunity to role-play interviewing. This allows the participants to get more comfortable with CBBI, and allows facilitators time to ensure that participants are maximizing the opportunities for gathering detailed, job-related information.

A Fast Way to Make the Conversion to CBBI

You do not necessarily need to start with a clean piece of paper if you are going from traditional or situational interviewing to CBBI. While it is best to start by identifying competencies for the position and then selecting behavior-based questions that cover an important aspect of that competency, you can take a shortcut. The shortcut is simply taking your traditional interview questions and converting them to CBBI questions (making sure, of course, that they are legal queries). Some of these conversions are quite simple to do; others may take a little more time and thought. Figure 2-1 provides a few examples.

Figure 2-1 Traditional vs. CBBI Questions

TRADITIONAL	CBBI
How do you deal with an angry, upset, or irate customer?	We all have to deal with customers who are angry, upset, or even irate. Tell me about the worst situation you have had to deal with.
What would you do if someone asked you to do something unethical?	Tell me about a time you were asked to do something that you felt was unethical.
If you could change one decision you made during the past year, what would that be?	Tell me about a work-related decision that, if you could, you would like to redo.

TRADITIONAL	CBBI
How well do you work under pressure? Do you handle pressure well?	Tell me about a time you were faced with stressors at work that tested your coping skills. Tell me about a time you did not handle a high-pressure situation well.
If you could live your life over again, what would you change?	Tell me about a work-related decision you made or a situation you handled where, if you had it to do over again, you would do something different.
How would you rate your communication skills, and what have you done to improve them?	Give me an example of a time when you were not as successful in your oral communication as you would have liked to have been. (Probing question: What did you learn from this situation that you have used to improve your communication skills?)
What kind of people do you like to work with (or have difficulty working with)?	Describe the way you handled a specific problem involving others with differing values, ideas, or beliefs.
What motivates you to put forth your best effort?	We all get assignments we really don't want to do. Give me an example of a time that happened to you and how you managed to get it done.
How do you go about determining your priorities?	Tell me about a time when you had too many things to do and how you handled that.
How would you work together on a project with more than two or three people?	Give me an example of a time where you needed to get people who have very different work styles to work cooperatively on a project.
What are you most proud of?	Tell me about something you did in your (last/current) position that you are particularly proud of.
What process do you use to solve problems?	Give me an example of a difficult problem you faced and how you solved it.
What are your strengths?	Describe a time when one of your strengths enabled you to be successful where you might not have been otherwise.
If you were a tree, what kind of tree would you be?	Okay, I give up! There are simply some questions that can't—or shouldn't—be rephrased!

Although there is no guarantee that converting your traditional questions into CBBI questions will work as well as starting from scratch, chances are that you will get significantly better, more accurate, more complete, and, well, more behavior-based (or performance-related) information from the candidate upon which to base your hiring decision.

Objections to CBBI

As with everything, specific objections can arise about this type of interviewing. Let's deal with the primary six concerns one by one:

1. CBBI questions are time-consuming to develop.

Yes, it will take a little time to develop the competencies, define them, select and customize the CBBI questions, and develop the rating scales. However, until the job changes, this will not need to be done again. Even when the job changes, it becomes a matter of tweaking rather than redoing everything. Also, as mentioned earlier, this book eliminates the significant research that needed to be done to come up with appropriate questions in other interview formats.

2. Word will leak out about the CBBI questions, and we'll end up with rehearsed answers.

It's always a possibility that this could happen. If that is a concern, one up-front solution is to select three to four CBBI questions for each competency and rotate the questions on a regular basis. The worst-case scenario is that you occasionally run into a candidate who has—or sounds like she has—a rehearsed answer. This is where your probing questions can become even more valuable.

It is relatively easy for most people to come up with a good story, but it's another thing to be able to answer probing questions well and get the pieces to fit together right in a falsified story. When the story is falsified, most people will start demonstrating rather awkward, uncomfortable verbal and/or nonverbal behavior. To distinguish whether this is nervousness or falsification, you can always ask another question or reword the question you just asked from a positive to negative format (for example, from "Tell me about a time when you did . . ." to "Tell me about a time when you did not . . .").

3. These types of interviews take longer.

Yes, they do. Here are your choices:

Choice A: Conduct a quick traditional interview. Since research has shown that they have less than a 30 percent chance of predicting job performance, your chances of making a bad hiring decision for an $80,000-a-year job, for example, are pretty high. Depending upon which reports you read, it costs between 30 percent and 250 percent of a position's annual salary to replace an employee. Let's say the cost to replace the bad hire is 100 percent (simply because it makes calculations easy). So it will cost you $80,000 to fill that job. With a 70 percent or greater chance that this was a bad hire, you will then have to go through the entire process again, resulting in a cost of at least $160,000 to fill the position (and that's assuming that the second person hired is a good fit).

Choice B: Invest time up front to determine the requirements for the position (technical skills, special skills, and competencies), design and conduct a skill- and competency-based telephone screening interview, and conduct a CBBI that focuses on competencies and demonstrated behaviors. Research has shown that this approach is upwards of 65 percent effective in measuring and predicting job performance and success as compared to traditional or situational interviews. While you still have $80,000 invested in the hiring decision, you're significantly less likely (less than a 35 percent chance) to be going through the entire recruitment process again in the next few months to replace the new hire.

Yes, traditional, situational, and brainteaser interviews are, typically, much faster. They are, however, potentially much more expensive.

4. If we hire technically skilled people with the required background and education, we can train them on the "soft" competency stuff.

There are positions for which this is true, but why would you want to go to the expense of training people when you could hire them with the competencies already demonstrated at a proficient level? Also recognize that while some competencies are relatively straightforward for people to learn through training or on the job (e.g., customer focus, presentation skills, written communication), there are quite a few competencies that are extremely hard, if not impossible, to develop (e.g., ethics, innovation, organization, motivating others, compassion). In addition, if you take the "train them after you hire them" approach, you need to consider that it will take from three to six months for the employee to integrate each new skill into day-to-day behavior. This could result in a significantly long learning curve before he is performing all aspects (technical and functional skills as well as competencies) of the job in a proficient manner.

5. Behavioral interviewing is too structured and doesn't allow the flexibility to react to individual candidate differences.

CBBI is a structured process—and one that increases the likelihood (if well developed and followed by the interviewer) of conducting a legal interview. It is not so structured, though, that it does not allow for the interviewer to gather relevant job-related information. The interviewer is free to ask legally appropriate follow-up or probing questions. Many organizations will also allow interviewers to solicit reverse information from a candidate.

For example, imagine that the question in the interview guide is, "Give me an example of a time you really listened to a person who was telling you about a personal/sensitive situation." The interviewer can ask probing questions to ferret out the details of the situation. Many organizations also allow the interviewer to reverse the question by saying, "Now tell me about a time you failed to listen well to someone telling you about a personal/sensitive situation."

Another example of the flexibility of CBBI is that most organizations will encourage interviewers to explore examples of a candidate's related competencies. For example, imagine that you work in a company where there are competencies of *teamwork* and *perseverance*. You have asked the candidate a *teamwork* question, and during the response, the candidate talks about the team persevering in the face of multiple setbacks. One of your follow-up questions may be, "You mentioned the team persevering through setbacks. What were the setbacks? What did you do to get your team through these setbacks?"

6. It takes too long to complete a behavioral interview.

Yes, it does take more time. But the reason is that you are probing for actual behaviors rather than hypothetical answers. Most interviewees are able to come up with a "right" answer to hypothetical situations fairly quickly. They know what they should do. They have memorized the process or the procedure. However, people don't necessarily do what they should do or what they say they will do. Determining how people actually behaved in a real situation takes a little more time, but gives you a much richer source of information to determine whether the candidate would be a good match for the job or not.

Why Use Competency-Based Behavioral Interviewing?

First of all, CBBI is more valid than traditional interviews. Research shows that it is three to five times more accurate at predicting a person's potential than traditional interviews. With the high cost of hiring (or replacing an employee terminated for a "bad fit"), that can lead to substantial cost savings.

Second, because CBBIs focus on actual past behavior—behavior that the candidate is highly likely to repeat—you are more apt to get a real-life view of how the candidate will actually perform on the job. This is more likely to result in a successful hire, which means:

- Increased productivity
- Lower turnover
- Higher morale
- Better quality
- Better customer service

Third, because it is a structured process, it helps interviewers stay on track and minimizes the possibility that they will ask either planned or spontaneous illegal or inappropriate questions.

Fourth, when it is done properly, it provides the company with a legally defensible interview process. Because competency-based behavioral interviews are structured and objective, they tend to be more defensible than other types of interviews.

Key Advantages of Using CBBI

From an *organizational* standpoint, CBBI, when done properly, offers a number of key benefits:

- It establishes an organization-wide, systematic interviewing process that supports the vision, mission, values, and strategic direction of the organization.
- Since competencies are observable and measurable, it allows for the gathering and evaluation of objective performance data.
- It ensures that only relevant, job-specific questions are asked.
- It gathers specific, real-world performance information upon which to base a hiring decision.
- It increases the likelihood that a fair, objective selection will be made.
- It increases the possibility of hiring the candidate who is the best fit for the position and the organization.
- It lowers the organization's legal risks associated with interviews, when properly used.
- It promotes objectivity when used in conjunction with competency-specific rating scales.
- Candidate answers are more honest and natural—rather than preplanned and memorized—enabling the interviewer to determine more accurately whether the candidate possesses the competencies for success in the position.

From a candidate's perspective as well, there are at least two solid benefits to the use of CBBIs:

1. There is relevance between the questions asked and the position. Even if candidates don't like behavioral questions, they at least see more value in the question than they see in questions like, "If you were a salad, what would you have in you other than lettuce?"

2. Even candidates with limited work experience have had life experiences. For example, when interviewing for a position that requires *adaptability, initiative,* and *communication,* most people will have had an opportunity outside of work to demonstrate these competencies.

3

INTERVIEWING CONSIDERATIONS

As you are building your phone and in-person interview guides, there are a number of factors to keep in mind.

First is the importance of hiring people who fit with your culture. When it comes down to hiring someone who is a great fit with your culture and team but is lacking in some learnable skills areas or hiring someone who is highly skilled but may not fit in the organization and/or with the team, it's always advisable to hire for fit. This chapter explores some of the issues around culture fit and provides some thoughts for weaving this into your interview processes.

Second is the importance of asking legal interview questions. Too often hiring managers think that conducting a legal interview just means not asking questions like "Where were you born?" The reality is that any question—including CBBI questions—can be worded in an illegal manner. In this section of the chapter, some of the basics of conducting legal interviews are explored.

Third is the proverbial search for "leadership competency" interview questions. If that's why you bought this book, you are going to be—at least initially—disappointed. This chapter discusses why there really isn't such a thing as a leadership competency, and it gives you some ideas on how to dive into defining what you are looking for.

Finally, this chapter looks at the value in asking for negative examples as part of the interview process. There is a saying that "if it's too good to be true, it probably is." This applies to many things in life, including job candidates.

Can You Hire for Culture Fit?

After an extensive and exhausting search, you finally found the perfect candidate for a position. He has the right experience and impeccable qualifications. Everyone who interviewed him commented on how well he responded to the questions and how on-target and insightful his answers were. Four months after he started, though, there seem to be some pretty significant disconnects between what the new hire is doing and expected behavior in the organization. Respected organizational leaders are telling you that he is rubbing employees at all levels the wrong way—and they give specific examples that concern you. While it's a key position in the organization, you've come to the conclusion that having him in place is worse than having the position open. He's just not going to work out, so you let the person go.

If that situation sounds familiar, then you have had experience hiring someone who is a qualification and an experience fit, but not a culture fit. So the answer to the question in the section header above (the short answer, at least) is yes, you can—and must—hire for culture fit. However, getting there is going to require a little thought and a lot of objectivity about your organization, its staffing needs, and its *real* culture (as opposed to the one you *want* your company to have). And your organization's climate is different than its culture.

But before I get into that, let's deal with the pundits that shout from the rooftops that hiring for culture fit is a terrible thing to do. I will admit that *could* be true. Anything done poorly can cause more harm than good.

One concern expressed is that culture fit means that you are looking for doppelganger employees, creating organizations that are devoid of diversity. Some believe that "not a culture fit" is code for the person not being the same race, gender, etc. as the average employee or the hiring manager. If the interview is done poorly, then yes, that is exactly what you will get.

No one will argue that an interview—of any kind—can be done in a way that supports hiring the just-like-me candidate as the best possible fit for the job and the organization. While it's sad to admit this, there are some companies in which this happens. But it primarily happens because senior leadership and human resources allow it to happen. This kind of behavior can be stopped—or at least significantly curtailed—by ensuring that hiring managers clearly explain—from a skills, knowledge, behavior, competencies, and/or core values perspective—why the candidate is not an appropriate fit for the position rather than accepting a general dismissal of the candidate. Additionally, a focused, structured behavior-based interview process that concentrates on knowledge, skills, behaviors, and competencies rather than personal (and potentially discriminatory) criteria will increase the likelihood that you are hiring the candidate who is the best fit for the position and the organization.

Another concern that is expressed is that hiring for culture fit often becomes a search for a new BFF, someone you want to have a beer with after work or someone you wouldn't mind being stuck at the airport with during a snowstorm. Again, I have to say that if hiring is done poorly, this can definitely happen. Let's face it, most of us would rather spend time with people we have things in common with than people who are different than us.

But a good interview process is structured in a way that asks questions and gathers information that will help determine whether the candidate brings the skills, knowledge, values, and behaviors that will drive individual and organizational success. Good interview questions will not help the interviewer determine whether he wants to spend personal time with the candidate.

An objection to hiring for culture fit is that it breeds groupthink because you are hiring people who think much like your existing employees and this is going to lead to organizational stagnation or a lack of innovation.

That may make sense with an organization whose culture rewards agreement at all costs, avoids conflict, reinforces the importance of being a "good soldier" and similar behaviors. But if your culture rewards and recognizes creativity, teamwork, collaboration, and similar values, I'm not convinced that the groupthink argument holds together. With values such as these, everyone thinking similarly is probably a good thing. We can look at companies like Zappos, Chevron, REI, and Southwest Airlines as examples of successfully hiring for culture fit.

A final objection I will put forth is the idea that you will be minimizing your attractiveness to millennials if you hire for culture fit because they want to work in organizations that have a diverse and inclusive culture. If your culture is staid, inflexible, and archaic, there is absolute truth to that statement. However, when there is a match between the organization's culture and the individual's values, that is not true. In Deloitte's 2016 Millennial Survey, personal values were found to play a significant role in selecting an employer.

A great example of an organization that has a culture that would be extremely attractive to some candidates is Patagonia, headquartered near Ventura Beach in California. The company believes that it's not only okay for employees to go surfing—or do other outdoor activities—during working hours, but also feels that it refreshes them and makes them more productive. This would probably not be a good culture fit for someone who believes that you're at work just to work, who thinks that fun plays no part in work, or who has a nine-to-five work mentality. Within a short time, they are likely to leave because "employees here don't take work seriously." However, hiring a millennial who believes that work and life should fluidly blend together would likely be a good culture fit. Patagonia's culture is also socially aware, which, according to Deloitte's 2014 survey, would appeal to many millennials who want to work for companies that have a strong social impact presence.

While every process has potential pitfalls, the advantages of hiring for culture fit—when done properly—are significant. The exact statistics vary from one research organization to another; however, they all agree that when there is a good fit between the person and the organization, the employee:

- Reports greater overall job satisfaction. While research varies, it shows that 50 to 90 percent of job satisfaction directly correlates to culture fit.
- Is more likely to continue employment with the organization. Leadership IQ[1] reports that the 89 percent of employees who

quit or get fired in their first 18 months do so because of a lack of culture fit.

- Shows higher job performance levels. According to a Society of Human Resource Management study, employees perform an average of 20 percent better, and according to a *Harvard Business Review*[2] study, they are 31 percent more productive.

Up front, let me say that getting a solid grasp on your organization's culture so that you are able to ask questions, which will help assess the candidate's fit with the culture, is not an easy task to undertake. I strongly recommend if you have coworkers with organizational development expertise that you get them involved in this process.

As you begin the process of uncovering your organization's culture, you may want to ask yourself questions such as:

- What are the company's stated core values?
- What is the company's stated EVP (employee value proposition)?
- What does your company show, by what it recognizes and rewards (or by what it mocks or punishes), about what its values are? (Note: This may be contrary to what you answered in the first two questions, but it is valuable information for this exercise and others.)
- What behaviors (the good, the bad, and the ugly) contribute to people getting ahead in the organization? (Yes, if misbehaving gets people ahead, and you like that cutthroat, back-stabbing behavior, then you need to admit it up front and hire for it. Better yet, you need to develop a more positive organizational culture, but that's another subject altogether.)
- What are the beliefs of the people in the organization?
- What are the unwritten (and generally unspoken) norms by which one lives if one wants to be part of the organization?
- What are the competencies for the organization, department, and position?
- What are the written—and unwritten—rules about work?
- What is the formal culture and what is the informal culture? (And when they clash, which one wins?)

- What are the stories that are being told to new hires, and do those stories differ between levels in the organization?

By answering questions like these, you are able to start getting a handle on what is *currently* happening in the organization and on what "successful" employees are doing. The next question is whether these are the behaviors and values you want to grow and foster. In other words, will they make the organization successful in the future? If not, which ones need to change?

Now, what are the top five to ten of these? If you haven't given up on the process at this point, you should have a list of the mission-critical culture fit items (be they behaviors, competencies, core values, etc.) for your organization. This provides you with the starting point to identify the questions that will help you determine which candidate will be the best fit for the culture.

Be honest about what you value and what you want in the organization. If you aren't, you are simply not going to hire the best fit for the organization. One organization sent very mixed messages about what its culture and values were all about:

Employees in a manufacturing organization were, according to corporate, out of control (think prisoners running the jail). The human resources manager they hired was told that the biggest contributor to the problem was that employees had not received the kind of training, coaching, and performance feedback they needed to be successful. (Training, coaching, and providing consistent, ongoing feedback to employees was a stated organizational value, and one that was consistently reinforced during the interview process.) It was felt that, if the HR manager focused on employee feedback, growth, and development, the plant would turn around. The HR manager had a strong learning and development background and came in excited about working for an organization where one of the values was to coach, grow, and develop employees.

Shortly after being hired, though, she was given a list of "poor performers" who, she was told, needed to be terminated. Interestingly, she had found a couple of the people on the list to be excellent performers. A few people not on the list had significant performance issues. When the HR

manager terminated employees on the list who couldn't or wouldn't perform at the expected level, corporate was supportive. However, when
coaching and training did not get the performance of employees who were
not on the list up to the expected standard, her ability to terminate the
employee was often thwarted. The answer was typically for her to continue to do more training and coaching for the employee because termi-
nating them violated their "coach and develop" core value.

The HR manager refused to terminate the good employees on the
to-be-terminated list because their performance did not justify termination. In addition, she continued to push for the termination of those not
on the list whose performance was below expectations (e.g., the hourly
employee who consistently "forgot" to clock out for lunch). After the HR
manager terminated a couple of the people who were not on the list, she
was terminated—without warning, coaching, training, or feedback—for
violating the organization's "coach and develop" core value.

The bottom line is that if you hire for what you say your core values
are, but your practices are different than these values, you—and the new
hire—are in for a very bumpy and frustrating ride.

Before you throw up your arms and decide that this is just too much
work and that you are simply going to know a candidate who is a good
culture fit when you see her, I will tell you that this is highly unlikely. As
noted by Kevin Kelly, CEO of Heidrick & Struggles, "40 percent of senior
executives leave organizations or are fired or pushed out within 18
months. It's not because they're dumb; it's because a lot of times culturally
they may not fit in with the organization or it's not clearly articulated to
them as they joined."[3]

Looking at culture fit from a different perspective, consider Warren
Buffett's decision to hire Todd Combs and to label him as the leading
candidate to take over his portfolio when Buffett decides to step down.
Buffett said, "He is a 100 percent fit for our culture. I can define the culture while I am here, but we want a culture that is so embedded that it
doesn't get tested when the founder of it isn't around. Todd is perfect in
that respect."[4] The bottom line is that if it's a good fit, it's as smooth as a
silk. If it's a bad fit, it will be as uncomfortable for the employee and the
boss—and many others in the organization—as woolen long johns.

Culture fit matters. When an employee's values are aligned with the company's, the organization's brand comes to life in the behavior and actions of the employee. And this is exactly what customers look for. It's what hooks them and makes them customers for life. Just look at Starbucks. It hires people who deliver a perfect cup of coffee *and* provide an experience that, regardless of which store you are in, is perfectly aligned with its culture and brand.

Zappos takes it one step farther and provides people with the ability to opt out of even applying for a job if their values don't match the organization's. Right on its jobs page, it says, "Please check out the Zappos Family's 10 Core Values before applying! They are the heart and soul of our culture and central to how we do business. If you are 'fun and a little weird'—and think the other 9 Core Values fit you too—please take a look at our openings . . . ." And if they do get hired and find that they are not a fit for the culture, Zappos will pay the employee to leave.

Justworks has a culture that it is very proud of and clearly states that it hires to keep that great culture. Early on, the company clearly defined its values, and it believes that "Hiring for values doesn't mean hiring people like you . . . . It's . . . . hiring people that share the same ideals, while also bringing individual perspectives, histories and approaches."[5] It uses interview guides with questions that relate to the company's values.

Despite the fact that more and more organizations are beginning to recognize that values and culture fit is critical, they are not necessarily assessing for fit or they are using tools and techniques that don't deliver the best outcomes. Beyond a doubt, the most important of the tools you should use to assess organizational fit are behavioral interview questions built around your core values and culture. You will always get better results with behavioral questions (if they are asked properly and if probing questions are used when appropriate) than you will ever be able to get with traditional, situational/ hypothetical, or brainteaser questions. This is simply because behavioral questions are designed to help you understand the candidate's past behavior (which is the best indicator of future behavior), and they give you an opportunity to determine how recently the behavior has been demonstrated (because the more recent the behavior, the more likely it will be repeated). It's important to understand how the candidate has actually acted (or performed) in different situations, rather than how they *might* act (or how well they know the "right" steps in how to act/behave).

You might want to start out the process by first getting an understanding of the kinds of cultures the candidate has worked in and how she functioned in those cultures. Behavioral questions that may help you gauge this include:

- Describe for me the best and the worst of the culture at [organization].
- What was it about the organization that you worked for that brought out your best?
- Give me an example of a time when you took a specific, concrete action that strengthened the culture in an organization.
- We've all worked for organizations that were challenging. Tell me about something that was challenging in the work environment of one of the last organizations you worked for. What made that challenging for you? How did you handle the situation?
- Think about the company where you most enjoyed working. How would you describe that company; what made it enjoyable to work there?

From there, you can blend culture factors into the overall CBBI interview guide. For example, if one of your core values is exceptional customer service, you may want to say, "Give me an example of a time when you truly delighted an internal or external customer." If the story the candidate tells you boils down to what your organization would consider *satisfying the customer* rather than creating a *raving fan*, then the candidate is probably not a good cultural fit. Figure 3-1 will give you some additional ideas.

Figure 3-1 CBBI Questions for Culture/Value Fit

VALUE	CBBI QUESTION
Respect	We all have more to do than time to do it in. Describe a situation, though, where you took the time to treat a person in a way that showed respect for them or their feelings.
Integrity	Tell me about a time when you fulfilled a commitment on time even though it required extra effort or sacrifice on your part.
Risk Taking	Give me an example of a time when you took action in a situation where the rules, policies, or guidelines were not clear.
Humor	Tell me about a time when the only thing that got you through a difficult situation was your sense of humor.

If you're working on changing aspects of your organization's culture, then your CBBI questions should focus on bringing in a candidate who already possesses the values and behaviors to help drive that aspect of culture. For example, say that you are working in an organization where there has been low accountability and responsibility demonstrated at all levels. The company has begun an effort to increase accountability and responsibility, starting at the leadership level and cascading down through the organization. As you interview new leaders, you would want to have an interview question that helps you ascertain each candidate's willingness to be accountable. One such question may be: "Give me an example of a time you accepted accountability for a problem or failure before anyone else even knew there was an issue."

To reinforce what the hiring manager should be looking for in terms of fit, it may also make sense to identify the factors the interviewer should be listening for to determine whether the answer is poor, acceptable, or great. To minimize the likelihood that culture fit is used as an excuse or opportunity to screen out applicants, tools such as a detailed behavioral anchored rating scale (BARS) or other rating scale should be used (see Chapter 6).

While interview questions will provide you with solid insight into the person's past work actions and behaviors, you might also want to look at factors outside the interview process to determine whether a candidate is an organizational fit. It's amazing how, in nontraditional settings, information can come to light about a candidate's true behavior. Take the following seven techniques, for example:

1. **This really isn't an interview, but . . .** This refers to the "casual" observation or drop-by. This kind of low or no-pressure interaction will often result in the candidate speaking and acting more freely, assuming the interaction has nothing to do with the interview.

   For example, at Southwest Airlines they give candidates special tickets when they fly them in for interviews. This alerts employees at the airport to pay attention to how the candidate is acting and how they are interacting with others to determine if they are a good fit for the service-oriented culture.

   Another example of using this technique would be to have someone drop by the candidate in the lobby to let her know that you are running a little late. Having the person relaying that message briefly chat (in a preplanned, structured way) with the candidate can be insightful because the candidate will probably not see that individual as a part of the interview process. Also, never underestimate the observational powers of your receptionist. Getting his impressions of how the candidate interacted with him, how the candidate responded to other employees, or how the candidate talked to customers/vendors in the waiting room can provide insights as to how she will act as an employee.

2. **Let me entertain you.** If affability, sociability, and similar characteristics are important for the position, consider having the candidate spend time with other employees in a social setting such as lunch or a fun event. Most people let their guards down in these kinds of settings, and you are able to see more accurately how they will interact with others on a day-to-day basis.

3. **If this were a real emergency . . .** Job simulation may be an appropriate tool for some positions. A well-structured simulation will help you see if the actions that the candidate would

take are consistent with what is expected in the organization (e.g., the candidate takes a "no prisoners" approach to a problem, but you have a soft, forgiving culture; you might also see whether the candidate will let a minor product imperfection pass or reject it).

4. **Testing 1, 2, 3.** Some organizations are now also using psychometric tests—measuring competencies, integrity, motivation, personality, etc.—to assess fit. While there are tools that can provide some insight into an individual's values and style, these tools should not be considered the be-all and end-all of organizational fit. Any tool that is created by human beings for human beings is going to be flawed to some extent. Psychometric tools can help substantiate what you have found, but my personal recommendation is that they not be the deciding factor in and of themselves. It's also important to remember that there are legal issues that can arise if these assessments are not reliable and valid or are not used properly.

5. **Am I seeing double??** If this is a multi-incumbent position, you might think about having one or two of your outstanding employees (technically and culturally) spend some time with the final two or three candidates. This could either be an informal conversation or, preferably, you could have the employees ask a few pre-scripted questions that will help them uncover some aspects of culture fit. A word to the wise, though: Make sure employees who are not used to interviewing don't start asking illegal questions.

6. **Use the fork on the far left.** For some reason, people are different when they are off-site and dining. A candidate may be perfectly polite to everyone she meets at the company but, for example, is patronizing or rude to wait staff in the restaurant. People in positions such as sales and others that have contact with donors, customers, or vendors represent the company when they are interacting. If a candidate is going to be too lax, stiff, sloppy, rude, etc. in their interactions with

others when they are dining, it's better to find this out pre-employment rather than after the fact.

Think about taking the cue from a CEO who, as part of the interview process, takes the candidate to a meal. His primary concern is the candidate's character. One of the ways he assesses this is by inviting the candidate to breakfast—but there's a twist. He arrives early and asks the restaurant manager to make sure that the candidate's breakfast order is wrong. He does this to see how the candidate responds. The CEO recognizes that there are always going to be mistakes that leaders will need to deal with. The key, though, is how they recover from them and get the situation straightened out.

7. **Walk a mile in my shoes.** Consider taking people on a tour of the building. This can be particularly useful in manufacturing organizations. Watch the people's body language (particularly their faces) as they see the various areas. Pay attention to how they interact with production floor people when you introduce them. For example, do they shake hands? Engage the person in conversation? Ask questions? If not, and these are important aspects of your culture, then they are probably not going to be good fits. I know a customer service leader who found out later that she was not the top candidate for the position; however, the incredibly positive way she interacted with the employees on the shop floor jumped her from the third- to the first-place candidate. It was a good hiring decision for the company and, over the years, her cultural fit resulted in a string of promotions from customer service supervisor to vice president of customer experience.

When you bring culture fit into the hiring process, everyone wins. You are almost always better off hiring someone who is a great culture fit but is lacking in some developable technical skills than hiring a technical guru who does not fit in to the culture. You can always teach people who are willing to learn new technical skills; however, you are not going to be successful trying to teach someone new values. No matter how hard you try, you are not going to teach someone integrity or honesty, for example. They are either going to bring it to the job or you're going to have to accept that you've hired a great technical person who has a lack of integrity and honesty in his dealings with others.

While there is no fail-proof method of assessing a candidate's fit with your organization, ask yourself, "Considering the answers the candidate provided—based on the behaviors that they report having demonstrated in the past—how well do the candidate's actions, values, behaviors, and beliefs align with those of the organization?" If you used one of the other seven techniques, ask yourself, "Are what I saw the person doing and heard them saying in alignment with what we expect out of successful people in this organization?" Your answer to these questions will at least get you headed in the right direction of selecting—and retaining—good culture fit employees.

Legal and Illegal Interview Questions

This material is not meant to be a complete review and presentation of legal and illegal interview questions. If you are unsure as to whether you should or should not be asking a specific question, it is recommended that you consult your human resources department or your legal department for guidance and advice.

While a book on competency-based behavioral interview questions might seem like a strange place to have a chapter on legal and illegal interview questions, it's important to realize that illegal questions can pop up anywhere and at any time, from the minute you first greet the candidate to the minute you drop them off by the front door at the end of the interview. They can happen regardless of whether you are asking closed-ended (yes, there are still people who ask these non-information-providing questions), traditional, situational, brainteaser, or behavioral questions.

In an interviewing skills class I was teaching, we were talking about the initial interview phase of building rapport—those few minutes of chitchat that help put the candidate at ease. I asked the class, "What do you talk about with candidates during this initial phase?" One hiring manager said, "Well, if they look old enough to have grandchildren, I ask if they have any and how old the grandkids are. Everybody loves talking about their grandkids!" (Pick me up, I just fainted.) Another person said she talked about the weather. Relief washed over me until the person continued and said that she warned the candidate that the roads don't get cleared very quickly in the winter. She then said, "I say that you need to have a really good car you can rely on to get you through the snow— something like a SUV. What do you drive?" A third person said, "I always ask about the person's weekend. On Monday or Tuesday I ask if they had a good weekend, and on Wednesday through Friday I ask about their weekend plans." That sounded pretty innocuous at first; however, I soon realized that there are quite a few answers that could be violations of Title VII of the Civil Rights Act of 1964 or Title I of the American Disabilities Act, including:

- "It was a tough weekend. We were sitting Shiva for my mother-in-law."
- "Really fun! My Phi Beta Sigma brothers and I had our annual weekend get-away. Just the guys—no spouses, no kids."
- "It was amazing. I took my son with me to a weekend seminar at our mosque."
- "I volunteered in the children's cancer unit at the hospital. It's my way of showing my gratitude for being a three-year cancer survivor."
- "This weekend, I'm taking off the prosthesis I use for walking and strapping on my running prosthesis. I have a charity fund-raising race title that I need to defend!"

As much as I dislike thinking about it, it is also possible to ask illegal CBBI questions. Most of them start from a job-related basis, but then they turn illegal as the potential for bias creeps in with the inclusion of protected information. Some examples are questions like:

- We all have a lot on our plates, and sometimes it's hard to balance everything. Tell me about a time you had to make a choice between your children and your job.

- Sometimes organizational policies aren't friendly to single parents. Tell me one that you didn't feel was fair to you and what you did about it.
- Give me an example of a company that you worked for that you felt valued and respected the unique perspective that you bring to the workplace as a [insert illegal bias, such as Muslim, transsexual, disabled individual, etc.].

In every one of these situations listed above, the intention is good, but the inclusion of protected information makes the question illegal. All three of the questions can be easily fixed:

1. We all have a lot on our plates, and sometimes it's hard to balance everything. Tell me about a time you had to make a choice between two different work priorities.
2. Sometimes we feel that organizational policies aren't fair. Tell me one that you didn't feel was fair and what you did about it.
3. Give me an example of a company that you worked for that you felt valued and respected the knowledge, skills, and perspectives that you bring to the workplace.

Ask This Instead

It's interesting to note that, according to CareerBuilder,[6] 20 percent of employers unknowingly ask illegal interview questions, and at least 33 percent of hiring managers were unable to distinguish between a legal and illegal question. That makes it critical to ensure that the questions on the interview guide are worded in such a way that the candidate is not being asked—implicitly or explicitly—to provide protected information. For example, you may be interviewing someone for a regional sales position that requires some overnight travel. The temptation might be to say, "This job requires overnight travel two to three times a month. Do you have someone who would be able to take care of your children when you need to travel?" To stay away from asking this illegal question, you might simply say, "This job requires overnight travel within your region two or three times a month. Are you available to do this amount of overnight

Figure 3-2 Rephrased Illegal Interview Questions

ILLEGAL QUESTION	LEGAL PHRASING
"Are there any religious conflicts you have with working weekends and holidays?"	"This job requires that you work every third weekend and two holidays a year. The holidays you will be required to work will vary from year to year. Are you able to comply with that requirement for the job?"
"I see you served in the military. We are a very veteran-friendly organization. Were you honorably discharged?"	"I see that you served in the military. What knowledge and skills did you acquire while serving that you believe will be an asset to you in this position?"
"How long have you been working?"	"This job requires that the candidate have experience doing Y (e.g., that the candidate have advanced Excel skills, such as pivot tables, using array tables, doing complex tasks that might best be completed with macros). Give me an example of a project that you've done that will convince me that your skills are at this level."

travel?" The person's arrangement for childcare (assuming the candidate even has children) is irrelevant. All you need to know is whether the candidate is willing and able to meet the travel requirements for the position.

For some positions, being able to get to the office building quickly when on-call is critical. Having someone who lives an hour's drive away could, potentially, be catastrophic. If this is a legitimate, legal requirement for the position, instead of asking, "How long is your commute?" you could say, "This job requires that, when you are on-call, you be able to be on-site within 30 minutes for an emergency situation. This would include things like _____. Will you be able to meet this expectation?"

Figure 3-2 provides a couple of additional examples of how questionable or illegal questions could be rephrased when there is a job-related need to gather the information in order to assess a candidate's fit for the position.

The Question May Be Legal, But Is It Informative?

There are also questions that are legal, but I have to wonder why you would use precious interview time to ask them. For example, "Have you ever been fired?" While you can ask that question, the chances of getting an honest answer out of the candidate is pretty unlikely, particularly if the candidate has been fired. The reality is, most candidates are not going to be honest about whether they were fired, and when you call to check the candidate's employment information, no company is going to tell you that an employee has been fired. The other concern here is that by asking this question, you may be passing on a really great candidate. For example, wouldn't you want to hire an employee who was terminated because they refused to do something that was illegal or unethical?

Now let's consider the question "Why should I pick you over the other people I am interviewing for this position?" Most interviewers ask this question to determine one of two things: (1) some specific knowledge or skill that the candidate will bring to the job or (2) the candidate's ability to sell you on what a great fit they would be for the position. The problem is that this question leaves everything up to chance.

If you're looking for the candidate to provide information about a specific knowledge, skill, experience, or ability, then you need to ask the candidate specifically about what you are looking for. If you're looking for someone who can sell themselves, you risk hiring a great talker who doesn't necessarily have the skills, knowledge, and abilities to back up their talk. Think about this question logically: How would the candidate know why he is a better fit for the position than any other candidate?

It's your job to ask the questions that will help you determine fit, and then, based on the information you gather, it's your job to determine if this candidate is actually the best fit for the position. If you're looking for something specific that you need the employee to bring to the position—a specific knowledge, skill, experience, or ability—then ask a specific question rather than wasting your time and the candidate's time by leaving it up to chance.

Another great time and effort wasting question is "Where do you want to be in five years?" Is there anything really wrong with me if, in five years, I want to be performing at the highest possible level I can in the position that I'm applying for? Does it make me a stronger candidate if I want, in five years, to be in a position two levels above my entry position? It is true that you should hire people with potential, people who can grow with the company, but this person doesn't even know what those opportunities are in your organization at this time. Additionally, you need to recognize that the average time employees stay with an organization has dropped over the years and is now averaging about three years, making this question moot in many instances. Figure out why you are asking this question, and then, if it is to gather some job-related information, come up with a question that will get the candidate to tell you about his past performance.

One final example, though certainly not the last of this genre of questions, has a couple of different variations. It could be "In one word (or three words), how would you describe yourself?" It could also be "How would you describe your current/former boss?" or even "How would you describe your current/former coworkers?" The alleged purpose of this type of question is to see if you will be a good fit for the position or the company culture. Allegedly, it will give you indications of the candidate's personality, confidence, self-perception, and work style. I'm not quite sure how a word—or even three words—would provide sufficient information to evaluate any of these things.

It's really easy for a candidate to throw around words they found in the job application as words that describe them. The purpose of the interview, however, should be to determine if the candidate has the necessary knowledge, skills, and abilities to be successful in the position, not the ability to remember key words from the interview.

If you absolutely cannot resist asking this question, then at least ask a solid follow-up question such as "Give me an example of a time you demonstrated _____ in a work situation." This will give you an actual behavioral example of the competency, skill, trait, or action that the candidate identified.

The Question May Be Legal, But Is It Logical?

I realize that I may get some argument on this, but I'm going to stay steadfast on the position that there are questions that may be legal and fun to ask but give you virtually no insight into the candidate's ability to successfully perform on the job. The questions I'm referring to are called brainteasers, which I addressed in Chapter 1. These questions are often more for the entertainment of the interviewer than to provide any real job-related, experience-based understanding of the knowledge and skills the candidate might bring to the position.

Let's face it, "What would you do in the event of a zombie apocalypse?" is not going to provide you with any information to tell you whether the candidate can do the job. Interestingly, though, it is supposed to give you information that will help you evaluate how the candidate may react under pressure. Likewise, "Do you believe in life on other planets?" is likely to tell you less about the extent to which they believe that anything is possible (the ostensible purpose for asking the question) and more about their belief in alien life forms. In one organization I worked with, a senior leader insisted that asking a candidate "How would you wrangle a herd of cats?" told him volumes about the candidate's ability to organize, lead, and motivate others.

I may be going out on a limb on this one, but why not ask a question that actually gets the candidate to tell you a real-world example of what you're trying to assess?

If you want to know how someone will work under pressure, try asking something like, "It seems like more and more people are feeling under pressure at work. Give me an example of a time when you experienced high pressure at work, and tell me about how you handled the situation."

Rather than worry about wrangling cats to determine if a candidate can organize, lead, and motivate, consider asking a question similar to "Give me an example of a time you needed to organize, lead, and motivate a group of very independent people to function as an effective team." This is likely to provide you with past behavior information, which will allow you to more accurately determine if the candidate has the necessary experience to do this in your organization.

Finally, rather than thinking that the candidate's belief in life on other planets will be indicative of job success, you can say, "Describe a time that you believed in something at work that others doubted until they saw the results."

The most important consideration around brainteasers is that, while they are legal, they may appear to be discriminatory. In addition, the relationship of these questions to the job requirements is nebulous (at best). This increases the possibility of the entire interview being legally challenged. Sadly, this is becoming more and more of a possibility as the line between acceptable and unacceptable interview questions narrows. If you're considering these types of questions, do so recognizing that one small slip could cost hundreds of thousands to millions of dollars. From that perspective, one might want to think twice about whether it's appropriate to ask a candidate, "If you were trapped in a blender, how would you get out?"

I Wish I Hadn't Heard That

From time to time, despite your best efforts, you will have candidates who share information with you that could be the basis for discrimination. Most often, this is not done intentionally or maliciously in an attempt to trip you up. Often, the information is provided by the candidate as clarification or explanation around an answer to a legal question you asked her.

It still amazes me that people will provide this information voluntarily. Recently I was part of a search for a director level human resources position. The candidates we interviewed all had recruiting experience and had been in human resources in excess of five years. All candidates were asked job-specific CBBI questions. One candidate, when asked "What questions do you have about the company or the position?" led with "I'm surprised you haven't drilled down on why I was only doing part-time consulting for the past year. Well, a year ago I got really sick and had to quit my last job . . . [additional details deleted]. Now I've regained my health and am ready to get back into the job market." In response, I simply said, "I'm sorry, but I'm not understanding your question about the company or the position. Would you do me the favor of rephrasing the question?" Another candidate responded not once but three times to a job-specific question with work-related stories that ended up leading to a comment about his spouse and his children.

When faced with situations like this, your only option is to not acknowledge that you heard this information and, most definitely, not to make any notation about having heard this information.

Three Keys to Help You Stay Legal

There is no magic bullet to make sure that the questions you are asking are legal (other than maybe to make sure you have a structured interview guide that your human resources and legal departments have approved and you making sure that you do not stray from the scripted questions). There are, though, three keys to keep in mind that will increase the likelihood that you conduct a legally sound interview.

1. **Ask only job-related questions.** When you focus on competencies, behaviors, and skills that tie directly to the job description, you're less likely to stray into illegal question territory. One "test" you can use is to show the question to a few other leaders and see if they are able to identify the competency, behavior, or skill the question is designed to solicit information about. If their answer doesn't align with what you want to uncover, you might want to revise and refine the question.

2. **Ask questions directly.** Don't beat around the bush, play games, or ask irrelevant questions to try and find out if the candidate can meet expectations. If you want to know whether the employee is willing to remove his nose ring and cover his tattoos to align with company policy, then state the policy and ask if the employee is willing and able to comply with it. Also, don't assume that the candidate is going to be able to read between the lines of a question and give you the information you're looking for. If you don't ask directly for information, you shouldn't expect the candidate to be able to read your mind and provide it to you.

3. **Ask questions that generate work rather than personal discussions.** Sometimes you find that you have things in common with the candidate, whether it's a particular personality trait, where you were raised, your opinions on a particular situation, or anything else that is not specifically job related. Regardless of how likable or interesting the candidate is, you're there to assess his fit for a business position, not form a personal relationship with him.

The Missing *Leadership* Competency

When developing competencies for a management-level position, it is tempting to include a competency called *leadership*. In this book, you will not find that competency. That is because leadership is an amalgamation of a number of competencies, rather than a single competency. To determine what those competency components are for your organization, ask, "What does a leader do in this organization that puts her above the rest?" The answers may include:

- "Recruits the best of the best; isn't afraid to hire people who are more knowledgeable than he is."
- "Is able to get a group of people to work effectively as a team; able to build *esprit de corps*."
- "Is able to get the best out of each of her employees; people go the extra mile for her."
- "Makes good decisions, even when there is insufficient information or little time in which to do so."

These comments are put together into individual leadership competencies within the organization. Using the above comments as examples, the competencies may be worded like this:

- Hires the best.
- Builds an effective team.
- Motivates teams and individuals.
- Makes effective decisions.

Soliciting Negative Incidents

Many competencies present questions that can be used to elicit negative incidents as well as positive incidents. In some situations, negative—or "failed"—examples of the competency can be of equal or greater value than a positive incident the candidate could relate. For example, if the ability to learn from mistakes is extremely important

Figure 3-3 Success and Failure Questions

COMPETENCY: BUILDING A TEAM	
Positive Incident	"Give me an example of a time that your leadership transformed a group of people into an effective, healthy, productive team."
Negative/Failed Incident	"Give me an example of a time when you were less successful as a team leader than you would have liked to have been."

on a particular competency, it might make more sense to solicit the candidate's real-world experience from a failure perspective instead of or in addition to a success perspective.

For example, as shown in Figure 3-3, using the success and failure questions together may help you ascertain a candidate's ability to effectively demonstrate the competency of *building a team*, as well his ability to pick up the pieces from a failed effort and get the team moving in the right direction.

You may also want to ask a failure question when you are getting the feeling that the candidate sounds too perfect. For example, if one of the competencies for Position X is *results oriented*, you may say: "Describe a time when, against all odds, you were able to get a project or task completed within the defined parameters."

Imagine that all the answers the candidate has provided have indicated that this is an incredibly strong candidate for the position. You don't believe anyone could be this perfect. This is the ideal opportunity to reexplore this competency in a contrary manner, saying: "Now, I would like you to tell me about a time when you were *unable* to get a project or task completed within the defined parameters."

As the candidate answers this question, listen for critical issues. For example:

- Were the roadblocks within or outside the person's control?
- What actions did the candidate take to eliminate or get around the roadblocks?
- Did the candidate miss early warning signs?
- How significant was the failure?

- How did the candidate discover the failure?
- What did the candidate learn?
- How has the candidate utilized what she learned from the failure?

While questions that ask for examples of failure—and what was learned as a result of a failure—are not always going to predict potential problems with this candidate, they should give you some significant insight into their willingness to share and take ownership of failures. They can tell you about the candidate's ability to learn from errors, his ability to apply what he learned to the same or similar situations and, possibly, even his level of emotional intelligence.

4

HUNDREDS OF INTERVIEW
QUESTIONS YOU CAN USE

THIS CHAPTER LISTS 701 competency-based behavioral interview (CBBI) questions, organized under 89 competencies. Once you have identified the appropriate competencies for the position, level, and your organization, your next step is to develop brief definitions of each competency that take into consideration your organization's culture. Once the definitions have been developed, you can then pick those questions that best determine whether a candidate can demonstrate the competency at the required level for your organization.

Because organizations have slightly different interpretations of what each competency means, the questions listed under each competency, in most cases, span a wide range of factors.

There are also questions that are worded differently but that elicit the same information. This, again, is designed to enhance the organizational fit of the questions to the culture and preferred vernacular of different organizations. It is important to read through each question and select the one(s) most relevant to the position for which you will be interviewing candidates.

While you can—and should—ask probing questions when a candidate's answer is incomplete, the questions you ask are typically contingent on the additional information you want to gather or clarify. As a result, you will not see, for most questions, specific follow-up or probing questions in this chapter. With that said, there are some instances where suggested probing questions are provided in italics. Note that these italicized questions should not necessarily be asked as part of the interview process, only as a follow-up in the event that you want additional information.

SAMPLE CBBI QUESTIONS:

Accountability and Responsibility

1. Tell me about a work situation where it wasn't clear who was responsible and you stepped up and took responsibility.
2. Describe a time that you forgot about a commitment you made to do something for another person in the company until that person asked you about it.
3. Every position has deadlines. Describe a situation when you were having difficulty meeting a due date.
4. Give me an example of a time you made a decision that you thought was good and solid but that turned out to be flawed.

Action Orientation

1. Tell me about a time you got enjoyment out of working hard on something.
2. Give me an example of a time you had to work on a project/task that you were absolutely dreading.
3. Give me an example of something you've done in previous jobs that demonstrates your willingness to work hard.
4. Describe a challenging project that you worked on.
5. Give me an example of a time that you had to act with very little planning.
6. Tell me about a time that you willingly took on more work even though you were already busy. *How were you able to get everything done?*
7. We all feel that we are unique in our accomplishments. Tell me an accomplishment you have had that you feel is unique.
8. Sometimes people will drag their feet in taking action on some-

thing, losing precious time. Tell me about a time you saw that other people in the organization were not acting quickly on something and took it upon yourself to lead the effort.

Ambiguity (Ability to Deal With)

1. Tell me about a time you had to work with conflicting, delayed, or ambiguous information. *What did you do to make the most of the situation?*
2. Tell me about a time when ambiguity was an obstacle to you getting a task or project completed. *How did you get around the ambiguity or make the situation unambiguous?*
3. Give me an example of a time when there was a decision to be made and procedures were not in place. *In the end, did you put procedures in place? (If not: Why not?)*
4. We have all been asked on occasion to perform a task or accomplish a goal where the instructions we received were ambiguous. Tell me about a time when this happened to you and specifically what you did.
5. Give an example of a time when you could not participate in a discussion or could not finish a task because you did not have enough information.
6. Tell me about a time when you had to complete a project or task on a strict deadline with little or no direction.

Analytical Skills

1. Tell me about the most complex or difficult information you have had to analyze.
2. Tell me about the task or project that you were responsible for that best demonstrates your ability to analyze information.
3. Sometimes even though we study the data from all sides, we make errors in interpretation of the data. Tell me about a time that happened to you.

4. Give me an example of a time when you caught a discrepancy or inconsistency in the available information that might have caused significant problems if you had missed it.

5. Describe a time when your logical analysis was seen as illogical or flawed by someone else.

6. There are times when there is an incredible amount of data and information to be analyzed. Tell me about a time you faced this situation and exactly what you did to boil everything down to what was most important.

Approachability

1. Tell me about a time when someone came to you with a problem. *Why did you choose the course of action you did? How did it turn out?*

2. Give me an example of a difficult problem someone recently needed your help to solve.

3. Give me an example of a time an employee came to you and was anxious about something.

4. Describe a time when you went out of your way to put someone at ease.

5. Tell me about a time you were able to establish rapport with a person that others referred to as "difficult."

6. Give me an example of a time that you were provided with information that enabled you to stop a potential problem from occurring.

7. Give me some examples of when someone remembered you after only a brief introduction. *Why do you think they remembered you?*

Assertiveness

1. Some of the best business ideas come from an individual's ability to challenge others' ways of thinking in a mature way. Tell me about a time when you were successful in challenging others' ideas.

2. Tell me about a time when your job required you to say how you

really felt about a situation. *Why do you feel it was important to be so honest? How did others respond to your clear assertions?*

3. Sometimes it is important to disagree with others, particularly your boss or team members, in order to keep a mistake from being made. Tell me about a time when you were willing to disagree with another person in order to build a positive outcome.

Budget/Cost Control/Bottom Line Contribution

1. Describe a time when your [overall/expense/capital] budget ended up being way off base and what you did about that situation.
2. Give me an example of a cost-cutting/cost-saving measure that you implemented proactively.
3. Tell me about a time that you found the cost of an item in your budget rising month after month and what you did about the situation.
4. Describe for me a time you needed to reduce a budget and the criteria that you used to make your determinations.
5. The cut that most people dislike making the most is on staff. Tell me about a time you needed to reduce headcount and how you went about making a decision on which positions or people were cut.
6. Tell me about a time that a cost/benefit analysis you did proved to be faulty.

Building Relationships/Understanding and Relating to Others

1. Tell me about a time where your ability to pick up on subtle non-verbal cues from another person helped you handle the situation effectively.
2. Give me an example of a time when you were able to understand another person's perspective, even though it was drastically different from your view.

3. Describe a time when your ability to detect and understand another person's motives paid off for you.

4. Give me an example of a time when your ability to show concern for someone was the foundation of a strong, lasting working relationship with the person.

5. Tell me about a time you were able to deal successfully with someone in a difficult situation because you had built a trusting relationship with the person.

Business Acumen/Understanding the Organization

1. Give me some examples of how people in other parts of the organization used your department or group as a resource.

2. Give me an example of a decision that was made in your area that had an adverse impact on another area or department.

3. Tell me about a decision you made that had an unexpected positive impact on another area or department.

4. Give me an example of a time when your understanding of your organization enabled you to get something you needed that you probably would not have gotten if you lacked the understanding.

5. Tell me about a time when you recognized a problem before your boss or others in the organization did. *How were you able to detect the problem before others? What would have happened had you not?*

6. Describe a time when politics at work affected your job. *What was the impact? How did you deal with it? If you had it to do over again, would you do anything different?*

7. Tell me how you went about learning how your current organization works.

Career Ambition

1. Tell me about your career plan and what you have done so far to accomplish it.

2. Describe for me how you have "made your own luck."

3. Give me an example of how you have taken control of your career.
4. Give me an example of a time you knew you had outgrown a position and it was time to move on.
5. Tell me about your greatest career achievements. *Why did you pick those examples? Tell me more about [one of the achievements].*
6. Tell me about a time you felt off track in your career progress.
7. Tell me about a time when you turned down a good job.

Caring About Direct Reports

1. Give me an example of how you have celebrated an individual's or your team's success in the past. *What was the occasion? Why was it important to celebrate?*
2. Tell me about a time when you were able to provide a direct report with recognition for the work she performed.
3. Tell me about a time when you missed an opportunity to provide a direct report with recognition for a significant accomplishment. *Why did you miss it? What did you do when you realized you missed it?*
4. Tell me what you have done on a consistent basis to ensure that your direct reports felt valued for their contributions.
5. Describe a time when one of your direct reports was under a great deal of pressure or stress. *What did you do in the situation? What was the outcome?*
6. Tell me about a time when you sensed that something was wrong with one of your direct reports and talked to him about it.
7. Give me an example of a time when you realized that one of your direct reports was overburdened with work. *What did you do? How did your action affect the situation?*
8. Describe a work situation that required you to really listen and display compassion to a coworker/employee who was telling you about a personal or sensitive situation.

Change Management

1. Tell me about the most difficult change you have had to make in your professional career. How did you manage the change?
2. Give me an example of a time when you missed the early signs of employee resistance to an organizational change.
3. Describe a time when you felt that a planned change was inappropriate. Why do you feel that it was inappropriate? What do you feel would have been more appropriate? How did the change turn out in the end?
4. Tell me about a time when you had to adapt to an uncomfortable situation.
5. Tell me about a time when you led a change effort.
6. Describe a time when a change effort you were involved in was not as successful as you or the company would have liked.
7. Give me an example of a time when you had to adjust quickly to changes over which you had no control. *What was the impact of the change on you? On your employees?*
8. Give me an example of a time when you helped a direct report or other person in the organization accept change and make the necessary adjustments to move forward. *What were the change/transition skills that you used?*
9. Describe a situation where you, at first, resisted a change at work and later accepted it. *What, specifically, changed your mind?*

Comfort Around Higher Management

1. Describe a time when you were able to provide a higher-level management person with recognition for the work she performed.
2. Tell me about a presentation you made to upper management. *What was it about? How did you feel about making the presentation?*
3. Give me an example of a time when, by speaking management's language, you were able to convince them to do something that they might not have done otherwise.

4. Give me an example of a time when, despite being tense or nervous, you were able to make a successful presentation to a higher-level management group.

5. Tell me about a time when, had you taken time to think about how a higher-level management person or group liked to receive information, you might have been more successful. *If you had it to do over again, what would you do differently?*

Communication (Oral)

Successful Communication

1. Tell me about the most difficult or complex idea, situation, or process you have ever had to explain to someone.

2. Give me an example of a time you had to be excellent at multidirectional communication in order to be successful at something.

3. Describe a time you used verbal communication to get across a point that was important to you. *Were you successful? How do you know you were successful/unsuccessful?*

4. Give me an example of a time when you were able to successfully communicate with another person even when that individual personally may not have liked you.

5. Give me an example of a time when you were able to successfully communicate with a person *you* personally did not like.

6. Describe a time when you were successful primarily because of your ability to communicate orally.

7. Tell me about a sensitive or volatile situation that required very careful communication.

8. Tell me about a job experience in which you had to speak up in order to be sure that other people knew what you thought or felt.

9. Give me an example of a time when you were able to successfully communicate with another person even when you felt the individual did not value your perspective.

Failed/Misunderstood Communication

10. Tell me about a time when someone misunderstood something you said. *How did you determine you had been misunderstood? How did you make yourself clear? What did you learn from this situation that you have used to improve your communication skills?*

11. Describe a time when you failed to communicate important information to your boss.

12. Tell me about a time when you failed to communicate effectively with your direct reports/client/customer. *How did you find out you had failed? What was the implication of this failure? What did you do about the situation? What did you learn from this?*

13. Tell me about a time when your dislike for an individual had a negative impact on your ability to communicate effectively with this person.

Communication (Written)

1. Give me an example of an important report you have written.

2. Give me an example of the kind of writing you do best.

3. Tell me about a time when someone misunderstood something you wrote. *How did you determine that you had been misunderstood? How did you make yourself clear?*

4. Tell me about a time when you had to use your written communication skills in order to get an important point across.

5. Describe the most significant or creative written presentation you had to complete.

6. Tell me about a time when you used your written communication skills to convey an important message.

7. Describe a time when you wrote a report that was well received by others.

8. Tell me about a time when you didn't document something that you wish you would have.

9. Give me an example of a time when you used written communication to share information that, in hindsight, you realize should have been shared verbally.

Compassion

1. Give me an example of a time you were particularly perceptive regarding a person's or group's feelings and needs.
2. Describe a time when an employee came to you with a personal difficulty he was experiencing.
3. Tell me about a time when you demonstrated to a direct report that you were concerned about a work or nonwork problem she was experiencing.
4. Describe a work situation that required you to really listen and display compassion for another person who was telling you about a personal or sensitive situation.
5. Give me an example of a time you had to put a critical task or project you were working on aside to attend to the needs of a direct report.
6. Tell me about a time when your failure to show compassion to someone at work was a costly oversight on your part.
7. Tell me about a time when you needed to give feedback to an emotional or sensitive employee.
8. Give me an example of a particularly difficult or awkward conversation you needed to have with someone.

Composure

Positive Incidents

1. Tell me about a time you took action based on your own convictions rather than giving in to the pressures of others' contrary opinions.
2. Describe the worst on-the-job crisis you had to solve. *How did you manage to maintain your composure?*
3. Give me a recent example of a situation you have faced when the "pressure was on."
4. Give me an example of a time when you worked particularly well under a great deal of pressure.

5. Tell me about a time you felt your team was under too much pressure. *What did you do about it? Do you believe, in hindsight, that what you did was the best possible action? Why or why not?*

6. Give me an example of a time when you had to think quickly on your feet to extricate yourself from a difficult situation.

Failure Incidents

7. Tell me about a time when you lost your temper/cool/composure.

8. Tell me about a time when you were knocked off balance on a work project due to unexpected information or an unexpected event.

Testing the Waters

9. Think about a time when you felt overwhelmed or stressed out. Tell me about the situation and how you handled it.

10. Tell me about a time when your work or an idea of yours was criticized.

Conflict Management

Positive/Success Incidents

1. Tell me about a recent success you had with an especially difficult employee or coworker.

2. Describe a time when you took personal accountability for a conflict and initiated contact with the individual(s) involved to explain your actions.

3. Give me an example of a time on the job when you disagreed with your boss or a higher-level manager. *What were your options for settling the conflict? Why did you choose the option you did? Were you able to get your point across? How successful were you in settling the conflict?*

4. Others' work ethics are sometimes in conflict with our own. Describe a time when this happened to you. *Were you able to work it out? How (or why not)? What did you learn from this experience? How have you applied that learning?*

5. Tell me about a disagreement that you found difficult to handle. *Why was it difficult?*

6. Thinking of the most difficult person you have had to deal with, describe an interaction that illustrates that difficulty. *Tell me about the last time you dealt with him. How did you handle the situation?*

7. Tell me about a time when you and your previous supervisor disagreed but you still found a way to get your point across.

8. There are always times when we disagree with others. Some people are congenial when we disagree with them, but that's not true of others. Tell me about a time when you had the courage to express your opposing opinion to someone who generally does not like disagreement. *What relationship did this person have to you? Why did you decide to speak up?*

9. Describe a time when you had to resolve a conflict between two employees or two people on a team.

10. Tell me about a time when you were faced with conflicting priorities. *How did you resolve the conflict? Was your solution effective? Why or why not?*

Negative/Failed Incidents

11. Tell me about a time when you did not properly handle a disagreement with a coworker.

12. Tell me about a time when you felt that a coworker or manager made you look bad.

Confronting Direct Report Problems/Issues/Concerns

1. Some people are more difficult to work with than others. Give me an example of how you have worked with the most difficult direct report and how that differed from how you worked with the most accommodating direct report.

2. Tell me about a confrontation you've had with a direct report.

3. Tell me about a time when one of your direct reports was not meeting expectations.

4. Describe for me a time when you let a problem with an employee get out of hand.
5. Tell me about a time when you needed to terminate an employee for performance problems. *How long between first determining there was a problem and termination?*
6. Give me an example of a time when you had to talk to a direct report about her performance and were able to turn that employee around.

Continuous Improvement

1. Tell me about a suggestion you made to improve the way job processes/operations worked.
2. Tell me about one of your workplace improvements that another department now uses.
3. Tell me about something new or different that you did in your department that improved customer service, productivity, quality, teamwork, or performance.
4. Tell me about a time you found and took advantage of an opportunity to make an improvement in your position or department/team/group.
5. Tell me about a time when you had to sacrifice quality to meet a deadline. *Would you say the sacrifice was worth it? Why or why not?*
6. In some aspects of work, it is important to be error-free. Describe a situation where you tried to prevent errors but were unsuccessful in doing so.
7. Describe a time when you caught an error that someone else made that could have affected the outcome of a project (or affected a customer).
8. Tell me about a suggestion you made to improve the processes or operations in your position or within your team.
9. Give me an example of a time when you improved the use of or return on a resource, where the positive impact was broader than just your team/department.

Cooperation

1. Gaining the cooperation of others can be difficult. Give a specific example of when you had to do that and what challenges you faced. *What was the long-term impact on your ability to work with this person?*
2. Describe a time when, had you not been able to get another person's or group's cooperation, you probably would not have been successful.
3. Tell me about a time when you cooperated with someone when you really would rather have not cooperated.
4. At times, we must all deal with difficult people. This can be a challenge when it is someone with whom we need to develop a cooperative relationship. Tell me about a time you were successful in developing a cooperative relationship with a difficult person at work.
5. Describe the toughest group/team/department from which you have had to get cooperation? *What were the obstacles? Why was it a tough group? What was the long-term impact of your actions?*

Courage

1. Describe a time when you had to make a decision that you knew would be unpopular.
2. Summarize a situation where you took the initiative to get others going on an important issue and played a leading role to achieve the results needed.
3. Tell me about a situation where you stood up for a decision you made even though it was unpopular.
4. Describe a leadership situation you would handle differently if you could do it over again.
5. Tell me about a time when you refrained from saying something that you felt needed to be said. *Do you regret your decision? Why or why not?*

6. Give me an example of a time when you needed to give constructive feedback to one of your peers or someone higher in the organization about his behavior.

7. Tell me about a time when you felt you needed to be assertive in order to get what you felt you or your team deserved or needed.

Creativity/Innovation

1. A lot of times we use tried-and-true solutions for problems and it works. Tell me about a time when the tried-and-true solution did *not* work. *Were you able to solve the problem? How? In what way was that solution different from the tried-and-true solution?*

2. Describe a time when you came up with a creative solution/idea/project/report for a work problem you had been dealing with for some time.

3. Tell me about a situation when you had to come up with several new ideas in a hurry. Were they accepted? Were they successful?

4. Tell me about a time you were especially creative in solving a lingering problem.

5. Tell me about a time when you created a new process or program that was considered risky.

6. Describe the most creative thing/plan/program/process you developed or implemented in your current or a recent past position.

7. Creativity often means stepping back from standard ways of thinking. Give me an example of a time when you were able to break out of a structured mindset and explore new or different concepts and ideas.

8. Tell me about the last time you thought outside the box. (*NOTE: Make sure they explain both why and how they did it.*)

9. Give me an example of when someone brought you a new idea that was unique or unusual.

10. Tell me about a problem that you solved in a unique or unusual way. *Were you happy with the outcome?*

Customer Focus

Effectively Handling a Difficult/Emotional Customer

1. Tell me about a time when you did your best to resolve a customer or client concern and the individual was still not satisfied.

2. Give me an example of a time you effectively used your people skills to solve a customer problem.

3. Tell me about a time when you encountered a customer who was complaining of poor service. *Were you able to resolve the issue? Why or why not?*

4. At times, we are all required to deal with difficult people. An even more demanding factor is to be of service to a difficult person. Describe a time you were successful in dealing with a difficult customer.

5. Tell me about a time when you wished you had handled an unhappy, angry, or irate customer a different way.

Building/Enhancing/Preserving Customer Relationships

6. Give me an example of something you have done to either develop or strengthen customer relationships.

7. Describe for me something you did to establish a "customer first" mentality in your department or team.

8. Tell me about a customer whose needs you spent considerable time learning about. What was the result of the time investment?

9. Tell me about a customer who has stuck with you over the years. What did you do to make this happen?

10. Describe a time you exceeded the expectations of a client/customer/stakeholder.

11. Give me an example of a time when you acted as an advocate for a client or customer in the face of resistance from a person or the organization as a whole.

Breakdowns in Customer Service

12. Describe a time when you were not able to deliver a product or service to your customer on time.
13. Everyone has said something to a customer that they wished they hadn't. Tell me about a time you did this. *What did you do to correct the situation? Did this satisfy the customer? What did you learn that you've applied to other customer service or service recovery situations?*
14. Tell me about a situation in which a customer was so difficult that you just gave up trying (or were unable) to satisfy her.
15. Sooner or later, we all have to deal with a customer who makes unreasonable demands. Think about a time when you had to handle unreasonable requests.

Miscellaneous

16. Give me an example of a situation you handled where even your enemies would have to say that you demonstrated outstanding customer service.
17. Give me an example of when you initiated a change in a process, procedure, or operations in response to customer feedback.

Decision Making

Difficult Decisions

1. Tell me about one of the most difficult (or one of the best) decisions you made in the last year/six months.
2. Give me an example of a time when you had to make a decision that required carefully considering a great deal of conflicting information, opinions, and data.

Rapid Decision Making

3. Give me an example of a decision that you made rapidly and one you took more time to make.
4. Describe a time when you had to make a quick decision with incomplete information.

Bad or "Do Over" Decisions

5. Tell me about the worst on-the-job decision you've ever made.
6. We all make decisions that turn out to be mistakes. Describe a decision you made at work that you wish you could do over. *What would you do differently if you could do it over again?*
7. Give me an example of a time you used a contractor or consultant for something that, in hindsight, should have been done internally.

Important Decisions

8. Give me an example of a time you had to make an important business decision that still affects you today.
9. Tell me about one of the most important decisions you have made when the information for that decision was based on the questions you asked.

Miscellaneous

10. Tell me about a time when you took a public stance on an issue and then had to change your position.
11. Describe a time when you had to make a decision that you knew would be unpopular.
12. Give me an example of a time when you had to make a decision and policies/procedures were not in place or there were no facts to guide you.
13. Tell me about a situation that, if you had not acted immediately, could have turned into a major problem.
14. Tell me about a time when you had to defend a decision you made.

Delegation

1. Give me an example of when you assigned an employee to make a decision or carry out a major task or responsibility.
2. Tell me about a task or project that you unsuccessfully delegated. *What happened? What did you learn? How did you apply what you learned to other situations?*
3. Tell me about the kinds of work assignments you give (or do not give) to your direct reports.
4. Give me an example of a time when you should have delegated a task/project, but chose not to.
5. Describe a time you had to delegate parts of a large project or assignment to some of your direct reports. *How did you decide what tasks to delegate to which people? What problems occurred?*
6. Give me an example of a major project or task you delegated to one of your employees. *How did you monitor the project or task?*
7. Give me an example of a time you did a poor job of delegating a task or project.
8. Describe a time you had to delegate a task or project to an employee who already had a full workload.

Detail Orientation/Attention to Detail

1. Give me an example of a time when your attention to detail helped you avoid making a mistake.
2. Tell me about a time when you caught an error that others had missed.
3. Describe a situation where you didn't pay as close attention to the details as you should have.
4. Tell me about a time when you paid too much attention to the details and not enough to the big picture.
5. Tell me about a project where you had the option to delegate the details or take care of them yourself. *Why did you make the choice you did? In hindsight, do you feel that you made the right decision and why or why not?*

6. Describe a time when you chose to focus on the big picture when you probably should have been paying more attention to the details. *Why did you make the choice that you did? What did you learn from your decision? How has this impacted similar decisions since then?*

Developing Direct Reports

1. Tell me about a time you had to confront and handle the negative behavior of someone who reports to you.
2. Tell me about a time you had to take disciplinary action with one of your direct reports. What led to that action?
3. Tell me about a specific developmental plan that you created and carried out with one of your direct reports who was not performing up to expectations. *What were the components of the developmental plan? What was the time frame? What was the outcome?*
4. Tell me about a time you had to provide constructive feedback to an employee who was not meeting performance expectations. *Why was the employee not meeting expectations? (NOTE: Listen for whether the person accepts responsibility for developing employees or places the blame solely on the employee.)*
5. Tell me about a time when you had to tell a staff member that you were dissatisfied with his work.
6. Tell me about a time you coached or mentored someone to a higher level of performance or a higher-level position.
7. Describe the steps you have taken in your current or previous positions to define and communicate performance expectations to your employees.
8. Many of us have had to deal with a situation where an employee was a good performer for a period of time, but then her performance started slipping. Tell me about a time you had to deal with this kind of situation.
9. Give me an example of a time you helped one of your direct reports develop or improve his (communication, negotiation, sales, etc.) skills. *How did you determine that this was a developmental need?*

(Providing) Direction to Others

1. Tell me how you know what your direct reports are doing.
2. Describe your procedures for keeping track of what is going on in your department.
3. Tell me about the process you used to set goals for your department and your direct reports last year.
4. Give me an example of a time when you failed to set clear directions for one of your direct reports or your team.
5. Give me an example of a stretch goal you set for a direct report. *Why was this a stretch goal? Was the direct report able to accomplish the goal? What did you do to contribute to her success?*
6. Managers quite often delegate major projects to their direct reports. Tell me about a time that you did that and how you kept informed about the status of the project.

Diversity (Valuing and Encouraging)

Adapting

1. Tell me about a time when you had to adapt to a wide variety of people by accepting or understanding their perspectives.
2. Tell me about a time when you adapted your style in order to work effectively with those who were different from you.
3. Give me an example of a time when a person's cultural background affected your approach to a work situation.

Different Values/Beliefs

4. Tell me about the most difficult challenge you have faced in working cooperatively with someone who did not share your ideas, values, or beliefs. (*NOTE: Make sure you understand what the differences were.*) *What was the impact on your ability to get things done? What was the impact on the other person's ability to get things done?*

5. Give me an example of a time when your values and beliefs impacted your relationship with a peer, coworker, supervisor, or customer.

Work Environment

6. Tell me the steps you have taken to create a work environment where differences are valued, encouraged, and supported.
7. Describe a time when you were able to make your voice heard in a predominantly opposite-sex-dominated environment.
8. Tell me about a time when you took action to make someone feel comfortable in an environment where people were obviously uncomfortable with his or her presence.

Miscellaneous

9. Tell me about a time when you avoided forming an opinion of someone based on his outward appearance.
10. Describe a time when, in a work environment, you made an intentional effort to get to know someone from another culture.
11. Describe a time when you had to separate the person from the issue when working to resolve differences.
12. Describe a situation when you had to give feedback to someone who was not accepting of others.

Emotional Intelligence/Awareness

1. Give me an example of a time that your ability to notice another person's feelings or concerns enabled you to proactively address an issue.
2. Tell me about a time that your ability to appropriately use empathy turned a situation around.
3. Describe a situation where, because you were aware of the non-verbal dynamics of a person or group, you adapted your communication and turned the situation around.

4. Tell me about a time you feel you mismanaged an emotionally charged situation.

5. Give me an example of a time when, because you failed to detect a person's feelings or concerns, you—at least initially—mishandled the situation.

6. Give me an example of a time when your understanding of your own emotions—and of the triggers that set off emotional responses in you—saved you from doing or saying something in a business setting that you might have regretted.

7. Describe for me a time when you were able to transform your anxiety or negative emotions into positive emotions and actions.

8. Give me an example of a time when—even though it was difficult— you were able to control and filter your emotions in a constructive way.

Empowerment

1. Describe for me a time when you provided your direct reports with the freedom to determine their work process, within the parameters of the task/project, even though you would have preferred that they do it another way.

2. Tell me about a time when you encouraged a direct report to make decisions within her area of responsibility that worked out better than you expected.

3. Give me an example of a time when you encouraged a direct report to make a decision within his area of responsibility that did not work out well.

4. Tell me about a time when you encouraged your direct reports to be actively involved in solving problems related to their positions rather than coming to you for the answers.

5. Give me a specific example of how you have empowered your staff to make independent decisions.

6. Describe a time when, even though it was difficult, you kept quiet and let a team resolve problems on its own rather than prescribing a solution for it.

Ethics/Values/Integrity

Personal Issues

1. Give me an example of a time when you were able to keep a confidence, even when you were tempted to break it or it would have been easier to break it.
2. Tell me about a specific time when you had to handle a tough problem that challenged fairness or ethical issues.
3. Give me examples of how you acted with integrity (walked your talk) in your job/work relationships.
4. Give me an example of a specific occasion when you conformed to a policy with which you did not agree.
5. Tell me about a time when you gave the benefit of the doubt to someone and were glad that you did. (*NOTE: This question also works well worded negatively: ". . . you did not give someone the benefit of the doubt and wish you had."*)
6. At times, we are all faced with the situation of having to tell a customer, employee, boss, or someone else "no" because we don't believe that "yes" would be the right answer—even though it would be the easy answer. Tell me about a time when you faced this kind of situation.
7. Tell me about a time when you took responsibility for a mistake before anyone else even knew that you had made a mistake.
8. We are all faced with having to make a choice between two seemingly opposing things, both of which seem like the right decision. Tell me about a time you were in this situation. *What did you do? Why did you choose that "right" action?*
9. Discuss a time when your integrity was challenged.
10. Tell me about a time when you experienced a loss for doing what was right.
11. Tell me about a business situation where you felt honesty was inappropriate. (*NOTE: make sure you understand why the candidate thought honesty was inappropriate.*)

Handling Ethics/Values/Integrity Issues with Others

12. Tell me about a time you saw someone at work stretch or bend the rules beyond what you felt was acceptable.
13. Give me an example of a time you had to present the unvarnished truth to someone, but were able to do it in a positive and helpful manner.

Failure/Regret Incidents

14. We have all done things that we regretted after the fact. Give me an example of a time when this happened to you. *If you had it to do over again, what would you do differently?*
15. Tell me about a time when you didn't practice what you preached.

Fairness to Direct Reports

1. Describe a time when you failed to treat all your direct reports equally.
2. Tell me about a time when you had to have a candid discussion with one of your direct reports regarding a work-related issue.
3. Give me an example of a time when you had to handle a tough employee problem that challenged your ability to remain fair to all employees.
4. Tell me about a time when you gave one employee preferential treatment.
5. Tell me about a time when you treated all your direct reports equally even though you were tempted to show preferential treatment to one or some of them.

Flexibility/Adaptability

Switching Gears

1. Tell me about a time when you had to stop working on a project/ idea/assignment and start working on a completely different one.

2. Give me an example of a time when your tightly scheduled day was interrupted and thrown way off schedule.
3. Describe a time when you changed your behavior to fit a specific situation. (*NOTE: Make sure you find out, at minimum, what the situation was, what the specific behavior was prior to and after the change, why the behavior change was made, and whether the behavior change was appropriate in retrospect.*)

Need to Modify or Change

4. Tell me about a time when you changed or modified your priorities to meet another person's or group's expectations or work style.
5. Tell me about a time when you had to change your point of view or your plans to take into account new information or a change in priorities.
6. Describe a time when you were instructed to modify or change your actions to respond to the needs of another person. *Do you feel that the demand was fair? Why or why not?*
7. Tell me about a time when you uncovered new information that affected a decision that you had already made.
8. Tell me about a situation in which you have had to adjust to changes over which you had no control.
9. Describe an instance when you had to think on your feet to extricate yourself from a difficult situation.

Failed/Negative Incidents

10. Give me an example of a time when you were unwilling or unable to make the necessary sacrifice to achieve a goal.
11. Most organizations today make ongoing changes in policies and procedures. Tell me about a time you had difficulty in dealing with one of these changes. *What about the change made it difficult? How did you deal with the situation?*

Follow-Up/Follow-Through

1. Every now and then, things slip through the cracks. Tell me about a time when you lost track of the progress an employee was making on a delegated task or project. *What were the implications? Were you able to get the project or task back on track? How (or why not)?*

2. Give me an example of how you followed up about the satisfaction of an internal/external customer/client whose problem you addressed.

3. Describe a situation or project you had significant impact on because of your ability to follow through.

Functional/Technical/Job Skills

Develop

1. Tell me about a situation in which you had to apply some newly acquired knowledge or skill. *What was the knowledge or skill?*

2. In your current (or most recent) position, tell me how you developed an appropriate depth of knowledge and skill about the company's products/services.

Anticipate

3. Tell me how you keep abreast of the professional/technical aspects of your position.

4. Tell me about a time when you anticipated the need to improve a technical/functional skill and took action proactively.

5. Give me an example of a time when you took the initiative to find out about a new or upcoming product/service change.

Contributions to/Application in the Organization

6. Tell me about a time when your industry knowledge enabled you to identify a potential problem and develop a strategy to address it. *What in your knowledge base enabled you to detect the potential problem?*

7. Through a real-life story, convince me that you are able to apply specific product/service knowledge to solve an internal or external problem.

8. Give me an example of how you acquired a technical skill and converted it into a practical application.

9. Tell me about your greatest success in using logic to solve a (technical/functional/job skill) problem. *Why do you think you were successful?*

Failed/Negative Incidents

10. At some point, everyone gets in over his head. Tell me about a time this happened to you.

11. Tell me about a time when you were unable to overcome a (technical/functional/job skill) problem. *Why do you think you were unsuccessful? What did you learn from that situation?*

Goal Setting/Accomplishment/Focus

Successes

1. Give me an example of a time when you set a goal and were able to meet or achieve it.

2. Tell me about a time when your department was going through long-term changes or working on a long-term project. *What did you do to keep your staff focused?*

Failed/Negative Incidents

3. Tell me about an important goal you failed to achieve.

4. Describe a time when you set a goal for yourself and did not achieve it because it was too high/too low. *What was the standard? Why was it too high/too low? What were the ramifications of your failure to achieve the goal?*

Processes

5. Describe how you set your goals for last year and how you measured your work. Did you achieve your goals? If not, why not?

6. Tell me about a major project you recently finished. Specifically, how did you set the goals and monitor your progress?

Challenges

7. Tell me about a time when you were given a goal by someone else that you believed would be impossible to attain.

8. Give me an example of a time when you made a major sacrifice (or were unwilling/unable to make a major sacrifice) to achieve an important goal.

9. Describe your organization's culture and how that culture made it challenging for you to achieve one of your goals.

Hiring/Staffing

1. Give me an example of a time when you were responsible for hiring and orienting a new employee. *What did you do to help her learn the new job? What did you do to help her learn about the company?*

2. Tell me about the best/worst hire you ever made.

3. We have all made what looked to be a great hire, but turned out not to be. Tell me about a time when this happened to you.

4. Tell me about a time when you discovered raw talent within your organization and recruited that person. *How did it work out?*
5. Give me an example of the talents and skills that a couple of your direct reports have that you don't possess.
6. Walk me through the process you used for the last position you filled.
7. Every now and then there is a position that is hard to fill. Tell me about the last time you had to deal with that. *Why was the position hard to fill? How did you overcome that obstacle?*

(Using) Humor

1. Tell me about a time when you used your sense of humor to diffuse a potential problem.
2. Give me an example of a time when you did something so silly that you had to laugh at yourself.
3. Describe a situation where you used humor to ease tensions.
4. Give me an example of a time when, in retrospect, if you had used your sense of humor, something at work would most likely have worked out better.
5. Tell me about a time when you used humor that backfired on you.
6. Tell me about a situation where you dealt effectively with another person's inappropriate use of humor.
7. Give me an example of a time when your ability to employ a sense of humor made you more successful than if you had not used it.

Influencing/Persuading

1. Tell me about the best idea you ever sold to a peer, employee, or higher-level management. *What was your approach? Why do you think you succeeded?*
2. Tell me about a time when you anticipated a problem and were able to use your influence or persuasiveness to change the direction of the situation positively.

3. Tell me how you persuaded someone to support an unpopular project or idea.

4. Describe a situation in which you were able to use persuasion to successfully convince someone to see or do things your way. (*NOTE: Make sure you find out what level the person was who was convinced.*)

5. Tell me about a time when you used your interpersonal skills to build a network of contacts to reach goals.

6. Describe a time when you had to influence a number of different people/groups coming from different perspectives to support you in what you wanted or needed to do. *What kind of influencing techniques did you use? How were the techniques you used different from one group/person to another?*

7. Give me an example of a time you had to convince others to conform to a policy, practice, or procedure you didn't believe in.

8. Tell me about a specific experience that illustrates your ability to influence another person verbally. Use an example that involves such things as changing an attitude, selling an idea, or changing a process/procedure.

9. Tell me about a situation where you had to persuade someone to accept your idea or proposal.

Failed Incidents

10. Describe a time you were unable to sell your idea to a key person.

11. Describe a situation in which you were unable to successfully persuade or convince someone to see or do things your way.

Information Gathering

1. Tell me about a time when your failure to gather sufficient information resulted in your making a decision or taking an action that you probably should not have done.

2. Describe a time when your patience in gathering information paid off.

3. Tell me about the most difficult time you have had in the last couple of years gathering the information you needed for a task or project.

4. Give an example of a time when, because you didn't have enough information, you felt it was wise not to voice your opinion on something.

5. Tell me about a situation where, because you had a strong network, you were able to gather information that others were not able to secure.

Information Sharing

1. Tell me about a time when you failed to give your team or a member of your team the information needed to do the assigned job.

2. Give me an example of a time when you provided a direct report with information that helped her make a good decision.

3. Describe a situation where you delayed providing others with information that would have been valuable to them.

4. Give me an example of a time where you felt you did an outstanding job of sharing information with another person.

5. Keeping information confidential is very important. Describe the last time someone asked you for information that they should not have access to.

6. Give me an example of a time when you were slow to share information with your direct reports or team members and this had a negative impact on one or more of them.

Initiative

Project-Related

1. Give me an example of a project where you came up with the idea and managed the process from start to finish. *How did you know it was needed? How did it work?*
2. Give me an example of a project or task that you had to accomplish without sufficient information, guidelines, or direction.
3. Tell me about a project or idea—not necessarily your own—that was implemented successfully primarily because of your efforts.

Initiating Change (Proactive)

4. Describe a situation where you responded proactively.
5. Describe a situation in which you recognized a potential problem as an opportunity and took action. *Did your action address the situation? Why or why not?*

Going Above and Beyond

6. Give me an example of a time when you went above or beyond the call of duty in order to get a job done.
7. Describe a time when you took the initiative to act rather than waiting to be told what to do.
8. Give me some examples of you doing more than what was expected of you in your job.
9. Describe a time when you took the initiative to do something that needed to be done, even though it wasn't really your responsibility. *What circumstances prompted you to act?*
10. We all have periods of downtime at work. Tell me about a period of downtime you had, why you had it, and what you did with that time.
11. Give me an example of an idea you tried to sell to management that was not adopted. *Why do you think it wasn't adopted? If you had it to do over again, what would you do differently?*

Interpersonal Skills/Savvy

Building Rapport and Relationships

1. Describe for me a situation where you had to build and maintain a new relationship in order to accomplish a business goal.
2. Building rapport with some people can be challenging. Give an example of a time when you were able to build rapport quickly with someone in your organization, even though the situation was a difficult one.
3. Describe a time when you were able to read another person effectively and, as a result, were able to adjust your actions to meet this person's needs or values.

Working with Difficult People

4. Tell me about a time when you had to deal with a rude (or sarcastic, know-it-all, gossipy, negative, uncooperative, finger-pointing, etc.) person. *How did you handle the situation? Were you able to get along? How (or why not)?*
5. Tell me about a situation where you had to work closely with a difficult coworker in order for you to successfully accomplish something. *Did you make it work? How (or why not)?*

Failed/Negative Incidents

6. Some people are more difficult than others to get along with. Tell me about your least successful working relationship. *Why do you think it was not a successful relationship?*
7. Give me an example of a situation where you misread another person and ended up making the situation worse instead of better, at least initially.

Miscellaneous

8. Describe a project you were responsible for that required a lot of interaction with people over a long period of time.

9. Sometimes it is important to disagree with others in order to keep a mistake from being made. Tell me about a time when you were willing to disagree with another person in order to build a positive outcome. (*NOTE: Make sure you find out who the person was she disagreed with, what the outcome was, and whether the outcome was positive—or if not, what happened to keep it from being a positive outcome.*)

10. Describe for me a time when you had to—tactfully but forcefully—say things that another person or group did not want to hear.

Learning/Knowledge Acquisition and Application

1. Tell me about a time when you had to learn something new in a short amount of time. *What created the urgency to learn? What did you have to learn? How did you learn it?*

2. Describe a time when you had to learn something quickly to solve a problem.

3. Give me an example of something difficult you had to learn that you did end up learning.

4. Tell me about a time when you had to do an unfamiliar task.

5. Tell me about a time when you needed to learn something quickly for a new task or project. *How did you go about it?*

6. Give me an example of a situation at one of your previous employers when others knew more than you did. *How did you close the gap?*

7. Walk me through the actions that you have taken to further your own professional development over the last six months/ year/five years.

8. Tell me about a job that you had that required you to learn new things.

9. We all have disappointing business experiences. Tell me about one you had and what you learned from it.

Listening

1. Tell me about a time on your last job when you had to get a project done with only oral instructions to guide you.
2. Give me an example of a time when you were a good listener.
3. Sometimes people hear but don't listen. Tell me about a time when you misunderstood someone. *Why do you think you misunderstood? How did you resolve the misunderstanding?*
4. Tell me about a time when you lost your patience listening to someone who you believed did not know what he was talking about.
5. Describe a time you heard someone out, even though you initially disagreed with the person, only to change your mind in the end.
6. Give me an example of a time when you had to deal with a highly emotional direct report.
7. Tell me about a time when your active listening skills really paid off for you.
8. Describe a work situation that required you to *really* listen to a person who was telling you about a personal or sensitive situation.

Manager Relationships

1. Describe a time when you were able to provide your boss with recognition for the work she performed.
2. Tell me about a time when you went the "extra mile" for a boss. *Why did you do it? Was it recognized by your boss and, if so, how?*
3. Give me an example of something that you learned from your boss that has helped you in your career.

4. Tell me about a time your boss coached you to improve your performance or to learn something new.
5. Give me some examples of the kinds of things you have talked to your boss about rather than handling them yourself.
6. Tell me about the worst boss you've had. *What made him the worst boss? How were you able to work with this person?*

Managing and Measuring Work Performance

1. Tell me about the methods you use to keep informed of your employees' activities, achievements, progress toward objectives, etc.
2. Give me an example of a time when you had to tell a direct report that you were dissatisfied with her work.
3. Describe your procedures for evaluating your direct reports.
4. Give me an example of a time you built a feedback loop into the work you delegated to a direct report.
5. Tell me about a major project you managed. *How did you assign tasks to your direct reports? How did you monitor progress? How did you measure success along the way and in the end?*
6. Give me an example of a time when you had to take disciplinary action with a direct report.
7. Tell me about a time when you were not as effective as you would have liked to have been in managing an employee's or a team's work.
8. Tell me about a time you needed to implement a new (or significantly raise an existing) performance standard for your team. *What was the standard? Why did you need to raise it? How did you communicate the change? How did the affected employees respond when they were told? Were people able to meet the new performance standard? If not, why not?*

Motivation

Self-Motivation

1. Tell me about a time when you were highly motivated and your example inspired others.
2. We all get assignments we really don't want to do. Give me an example of a time when that happened to you, and tell me how you motivated yourself to get it done.

Motivating Others

3. Relate a scenario where you were responsible for motivating others.
4. Give me an example of a time of low morale when you were able to motivate another person or group to achieve something that they weren't really motivated to achieve.
5. Tell me about a time when you provided your team or direct reports with the things they needed to motivate themselves to an extraordinary accomplishment.
6. Tell me about a time when you were able to give an employee what he needed to maintain or regain his motivation.
7. Tell me about a time when you had to handle a tough morale problem.

Negotiation

1. Tell me about a time when you gained acceptance of an idea or project from your boss. *How did you get this acceptance?*
2. Give me an example of an approach you used to sell an idea to an employee, peer, or someone higher in management.
3. Describe for me a situation where two individuals or parties were at odds, and you helped negotiate a win-win solution.
4. Tell me about a time when you needed to get cooperation from someone in another department for you to be successful on a task or project.

5. Tell me about the most important negotiation you have handled in the last couple of years.
6. Tell me about a time that you were successful in a negotiation because you backed off of something that was part of the negotiation.
7. Tell me about a time you were unsuccessful in a negotiation because you chose not to back off of something that was part of the negotiation.
8. Give me an example of a time when you were unhappy with the results of a negotiation you were involved in.
9. Tell me about a time you won (or lost) an important contract.

(Removing) Obstacles

1. Give me an example of a time when you helped an employee or a team succeed by removing an obstacle in its path.
2. Tell me about a time when a significant obstacle stood in your path to success. How were you able to remove the obstacle (or why were you unable to remove the obstacle)?
3. Describe a project you had where you had to overcome multiple obstacles in order to be successful. (*NOTE: Make sure you find out what the obstacles were and what the person did to remove or minimize them.*)
4. Tell me about a time that an obstacle was so significant that it blocked your ability to be successful.

Organization

1. Tell me about a time you had to handle multiple responsibilities. *How did you organize the work you needed to do?*
2. Give me some examples of how you determine priorities in scheduling your time.
3. With fax machines, email, and other technology speeding up processes, time still seems to be something we are always lacking.

Describe some things you have done to organize your work in the past to meet the various time demands.

4. Tell me about a time when you were particularly effective in prioritizing tasks and completing a project on schedule.

5. Tell me about one of your best accomplishments, including where the assignment came from, your plans in carrying it out, how you eventually did carry it out, and any obstacles you overcame.

6. Give me an example of a time when you had to juggle several important activities and projects in a limited amount of time. *Did you stay on top of all of them? How?*

7. Describe how you have improved the organization of a system, process, or task in your current position.

8. Tell me about a time you had multiple tasks or projects given to you at the same time and how you decided what to do when.

9. Tell me about a time you got bogged down in the details of a project.

10. Tell me about the last time you missed a deadline because you were not well organized.

Organizational Agility/Awareness

Positive Examples

1. Tell me about a time when you needed to accomplish something through an informal network.

2. Describe a time when your ability to understand an organization's culture helped you develop the relationships and partnerships you needed to accomplish something that had to be done.

3. Tell me about the organizational climate at your current (or most recent) employer and give me an example of how that climate made it difficult for you to successfully accomplish a goal or project.

4. Give me an example of a time when your ability to read an organization's culture enabled you to be successful at something.

5. Tell me about a time you were able to accomplish something that was important to you through the use of your informal network.

Failed/Negative Examples

6. Give me an example of a time when, if you had taken more time to understand how your organization worked, you might have been more successful.
7. Tell me about a time when you misread an organization's culture.
8. Give me an example of a time when, had you understood the reasoning behind a key policy, practice, or procedure, you would have done something differently.

Partnering (Internal/External)

1. Describe for me a time when you developed and maintained (or strengthened) a relationship with a person or group inside your organization. *Why did you develop/strengthen the relationship? How did you do it? What do you do to maintain/strengthen it?*
2. Give me an example of a time you developed and maintained (or strengthened) a relationship with a person or group outside the organization. *Why did you develop/strengthen the relationship? How did you do it? What did you do to maintain/strengthen it?*
3. Most things we do have an impact on others—whether we realize it or not. Tell me about a time when you realized that your project could have a far-reaching impact, and you sought out relevant people to gather their concerns and perspectives before you proceeded with the task.
4. Tell me about a time when you got involved in a cross-functional activity simply to develop a better working relationship with those involved in the activity.
5. Give me an example of a time when you wished you had spent some time looking for common ground with stakeholders before you took a particular action.

6. Describe for me a time when you might have been more successful at something had you taken the time to clarify the expectations in a working relationship.
7. Tell me about a time when you failed to put in the required effort to maintain an internal or external working relationship.

Patience

1. Tell me about a time when you lost your patience listening to someone who you believed did not know what he was talking about.
2. Give me an example of a time where you felt that a process was getting in your way of getting something done.
3. Describe a process or procedure that guides your actions, but for which you have little patience.
4. Tell me about a time when you failed to gather sufficient information before acting.
5. Give me an example of a time when you misjudged a person or data.
6. Give me an example of a specific occasion when you conformed to a policy with which you did not agree. *Why did you comply? What would have been the consequences of noncompliance?*
7. Tell me about the biggest error in judgment you've made in your current position. *Why did you make the error? How did you correct it?*

Peer Relations

1. Describe a time when you were able to provide a peer or higher -level management person with recognition for the work she performed.
2. Give me an example of a time when you had a disagreement with one of your peers, but were able to find common ground and solve the problem.

3. Tell me about a time when you needed to gain the trust and support of one of your peers in order to be successful on something.
4. Describe a time when you had to give candid feedback to one of your peers.
5. Give me an example of a time when you were a team player in a project with your peers.
6. Tell me about a time when you had to deal with a coworker who was very upset.

Perseverance

General

1. Tell me about a time when you stayed with an idea or project for longer than anyone expected you to.
2. Tell me about a time when you finished a job even though everyone else had given up.
3. Tell me about a time when you encountered significant resistance or a major setback on a project you were working on, but managed to work through it anyway.
4. Describe a time when you were asked to complete a difficult task or project where the odds were against you. *Were you successful? What did you learn from the experience?*
5. Tell me about a really tough day that you had recently and what you did to get through it.
6. Describe a situation where you had to get a job done in spite of an unforeseen problem.
7. Describe your most challenging project or situation and how you overcame the obstacles.
8. Summarize a time when your persistence or tenacity had a big payoff.

Failed/Negative Incidents

9. Tell me about a time when you were unable initially to sell an idea to your boss, an employee, or a peer, and so you tried again. *What did you do differently the second or third time?*

10. Give me an example of a time when you gave up on something before you finished. *Why did you give up?*

11. Give me an example of a time when you tried to accomplish something and failed. *Why did you fail? If you had it to do over again, what would you do differently?*

Personal Growth and Development

Self-Awareness and Reflection

1. Think about a time when setting a positive example had a highly beneficial impact on people you worked with. *How did you determine that a strong example was needed? What did you do? What was the effect on the people?*

2. Tell me the one thing about you as an employee that you hope your current or last boss doesn't tell me during a reference call.

3. Tell me about a time when you were not pleased with (or were disappointed in) your performance.

4. Tell me about a time when one of your weaknesses got the better of you.

5. Describe a work situation that brought out the worst in you. *Why did it bring out the worst in you? What did you learn?*

Lessons Learned

6. Give me an example of a time that you failed at something (or made a mistake) and learned. *What did you learn? How did you apply that learning?*

7. Tell me about a time when you were asked to complete a difficult assignment even though the odds were against you. *What did you learn from that experience?*

Self-Improvement

8. We all have weaknesses that can interfere with our success. Tell me about one of yours and how you overcame it to be successful on a specific task or project.

9. Give me an example of something that you have done in the past to improve yourself.

10. Describe a situation in which you received constructive feedback about your work. *What was the feedback about? What was your assessment of the feedback? What did you do with the information you received? What changes did you make?*

Perspective

1. Tell me about a time when your ability to think globally/broadly/strategically or look at the big picture stopped you or someone else from doing something that would have been a mistake.

2. Tell me about a time when you had tunnel vision when looking at a project, issue, or problem.

3. Give me an example of a time when you were able to pose a variety of future scenarios to ensure that the proper course of action was taken.

4. Describe a time for me when you were able to solve a business problem or challenge by applying something that you learned through a personal or business interest of yours.

5. Tell me about a time when your ability to explore "what if . . ." scenarios enabled you to prevent a significant/major problem from occurring.

Planning/Priority Setting

General

1. Give me an example of a change you saw coming and how you planned for it.
2. Give me an example of an important goal that you had set for your team and the team's success in reaching it.
3. Give me an example of a time you had a lot of tasks put on your plate all at once. *How did you decide what tasks to do and when to do them?*
4. Tell me about a big work project that you had to plan.
5. Tell me about your current top priorities. *How did you determine that they should be your top priorities?*
6. Give me an example of a time when you were effective in doing away with the constant emergencies and surprises in your work environment.
7. Give me an example of a time when your schedule was suddenly interrupted and your plans for the day completely changed.
8. Think about the assignments you completed over the past few months. Tell me about the one that required the greatest amount of effort with regard to planning and organizing.

Failed/Negative Incidents

9. Give me a specific example of a time when you did not meet a deadline.
10. Describe a time when your plan didn't work out. *Why didn't it work? What did you do to recover? Were you successful then? If you had to do it over again, what would you do differently? What did you learn from this? How have you applied what you learned?*

Political Awareness/Savvy

1. Describe a politically sensitive situation that you were in and how you handled it.

2. Tell me about a time when you consciously chose not to play corporate politics.
3. Give me an example of a complex political situation you were able to handle effectively and quietly, which, had you not handled it well, could have blown up.
4. Describe a time when you agreed to implement someone else's idea over your own. *How did you feel about it? Was it a successful implementation? Why or why not?*
5. Describe a time when you were able to anticipate a land mine and plan your upcoming actions accordingly.
6. Tell me about a time when your willingness to play politics made you successful.
7. Describe a time when politics at work affected your job. *How did you handle the situation? Were you successful?*
8. Give me an example of a time when you used your political savvy to push something through for approval.

Failures/Learning from Failures

9. Tell me about a time when you unknowingly stepped on a political land mine. *What contributed to this misstep? Was it resolved effectively? How?*
10. Tell me about a time when you were unable to successfully navigate through a political situation.

Presentation Skills

1. Tell me about a presentation you made to a large audience. *What was the purpose? How did you prepare it?*
2. Give me an example of a presentation you did for a small group that resulted in the group agreeing to do what you wanted.
3. Describe a situation where, after a presentation, you were faced with a hostile questioner. *What did you do? What were the results?*

4. Give me an example of a time when a presentation you were making wasn't working and you were able to switch tactics to make it work. *How did you know the presentation wasn't working?*

5. Tell me about an oral presentation you made to a group within the last year. *What was the most difficult aspect of the presentation?*

6. Describe the most creative oral presentation you have had to make.

7. Describe the most significant presentation you have had to complete.

8. Tell me about a time you had to use your presentation skills to influence someone's opinion.

Problem Solving

Gathering/Analyzing/Using Facts and Information

1. Give me an example of a time when you used your fact-finding skills to solve a problem.

2. Tell me about a situation where the analysis that you performed was incorrect. *If you had it to do over again, what would you do differently?*

Catching Problems Early

3. We can sometimes identify a small problem and fix it before it becomes a major problem. Give me an example of how you have done this.

4. Describe a time you failed to anticipate a potential problem and develop preventative measures.

Miscellaneous

5. Give me an example of one of the most creative solutions you have come up with for a difficult problem.

6. Tell me about the most difficult problem you've ever had to solve. *What steps did you take to tackle it? Were the steps successful? Over what period of time?*

7. Solving a problem often necessitates evaluation of alternate solutions. Give me an example of a time when you actively defined several solutions to a single problem. (*NOTE: Make sure they talk about the tools used—e.g., research, brainstorming—as well as how and why they used the tools.*)

8. Tell me about a stubborn or recurring problem you are facing in your current position. *What have you done to solve it? Has the solution been effective? Over what period of time?*

9. Tell me about a time you had to solve a problem with no rules, guidelines, or policies in place to guide you.

10. Tell me about a difficult problem you solved that had a significant positive impact on all or part of the organization.

Failed/Negative Incidents

11. Tell me about a problem that got out of control before you discovered it and began working on a solution.

12. Tell me about a time you missed an obvious solution to a problem.

Process Management

1. Tell me about the process you used last year (or this year) to set your department goals. *Were the goals accomplished?*

2. Tell me about your system for controlling errors in your work.

3. Walk me through a recent project or assignment you completed, and tell me the process you used to ensure it was complete and accurate.

4. Give me an example of a situation where you improved a work process.

5. Tell me about a time when you took a complicated, technical process and explained it to people who were not familiar with the process.

6. Tell me about a significant project that you managed, focusing on how you made sure that everything was getting done correctly and properly.

7. Give me an example of a time when you saw an opportunity to integrate two or more processes or procedures to make a more efficient and effective single process or procedure.

8. Tell me about a situation where you found a way to get the job done faster and better at a lower cost.

Recognition and Reward

1. Tell me about a time when you used a prize, contest, or other financial reward to motivate a team or group. *Why did you take that approach? Was the approach successful? Why or why not?*

2. Describe a time when you were able to successfully use a competition between teams or departments to drive organizational success. *Why did you decide to use a competition? Did it have the intended effect? If not, what do you feel went wrong?*

3. Give me an example of a time when your ability to recognize others gave the team or individuals what they needed to keep themselves motivated to finish a task or project.

4. Describe a time when your ability to recognize progress, efforts, and contributions spurred a demoralized team or person to pick up the pieces and be successful.

5. Walk me through a time where you should have given someone recognition for what they did, but failed to do it. *Why did you fail to give the recognition? How did you realize you failed? What did you do when you realized you failed? What did you learn from the situation? How have you used what you learned?*

Resource Management

1. We all have more on our plate than we have time to get done. Tell me about a time when your ability to accurately scope out time requirements for tasks and projects made you successful.

2. Tell me about a time when you prepared a budget larger than any you had ever done before. *Did you meet the budget? What was the variance? Did the budget need to be altered (if so, how and why)?*

3. Describe a time you had to manage a project where the acquisition, storage, and use of materials were critical factors (e.g., the product had a short shelf life).

4. Give me an example of a time when you underestimated a resource you needed to get a task or project done, but managed to overcome the shortage and be successful.

5. Tell me about a time when you were off target on assessing the human resources you needed for a project. *Why were you off target? Were you able to rectify the situation? How did the oversight impact the project?*

6. Describe a time when you had to deal with a particularly difficult resource management issue regarding people/material/assets.

7. We have all faced situations where the resources we needed to be successful were not within our span of control. Tell me about a project or goal where this was true for you.

8. Sometimes the only way people or departments can accomplish their individual goals is to form a partnership. Tell me about a time when, had you not partnered, your individual goals might not have been achieved.

(Sourcing, Allocating, and Managing) Resources

1. When we start a new job, we can inherit some interesting resource challenges. Tell me about a time when this happened to you.

2. Tell me about a time when you had to deal with a negative budget variance.

3. Tell me a story that will convince me that you can handle even the most difficult vendors.

4. Give me an example of a time that, due to forces outside of your control, you realized you were going to end up with a shortfall of resources on a major project.

5. When budgets are cut, we also have to reevaluate which projects

get priority for the remaining resources. Give me an example of when you had to go through this, and walk me through the process you used.

(Showing) Respect

1. Tell me about a time when you had to resolve a difference of opinion with a coworker/customer/supervisor. *How do you feel you showed respect for that person?*
2. Tell me about a time when you needed to give feedback to an employee who was emotional or sensitive about a problem.
3. Describe the way you handled a specific problem involving others with differing values, ideas, or beliefs in your current/previous job.
4. Describe a work situation that required you to really listen to and display compassion for a coworker/employee who was telling you about a personal or sensitive issue.
5. Give me an example of a time when you disagreed with the views of your direct reports.
6. Tell me about a time you had to handle a highly emotional person.
7. Describe for me a time when you saw a situation very differently from someone else and disagreed strongly with him, but still respected his viewpoint.
8. Give me an example of a time that you felt you were not treated with respect, but did not give in to the temptation to treat the other person disrespectfully.
9. Describe a time when you recognized that you needed to respect another person's values even though they were significantly different from yours.
10. Give me an example of a time when, in order to be successful, you needed to work closely with someone you did not respect.
11. Walk me through a time when your belief in always showing respect for others enabled you to solve a problem with a supervisor/coworker/employee/customer who was acting disrespectfully.

Results Orientation

1. Give me an example of an important goal you have had and how you succeeded in achieving it.
2. Describe a time when, against all odds, you were able to get a project or task completed within the defined parameters.
3. Tell me about a time when you were asked to complete a difficult assignment and the odds were against you. *What did you learn from the experience?*
4. Tell me about a time when you had to pay close attention to the tiny details in order to be successful.
5. Being successful takes more than luck—it also takes hard work. Tell me about a time when you had to work very hard and make personal sacrifices to help your organization/department/team reach its goals.

Failed/Negative Incidents

6. Give me an example of a time when you were unable to complete a project on time.
7. Tell me about a time when you did not achieve the results you should have or in the required time frame.
8. Describe a situation where, due to time and resource constraints, you submitted a report or completed a project where the quality was compromised.

Risk Taking

1. Tell me about a time when, with an internal or external customer, you had to try something you've never done before.
2. Give me an example of a time when you felt that it was necessary or appropriate to circumvent company policy to meet a customer's needs.
3. Describe for me the riskiest business decision you have ever made. *Why did you make the decision? Were you successful and why or why not?*

4. Describe a work-related risk you took that, in hindsight, you wish you had not taken.

5. Tell me about a time when you created a new process or program that was considered risky. *Why was it risky?*

6. Give me an example of a time when there was a decision to be made and procedures or policies were not in place. *Was there a policy/procedure developed? By whom? How long after the situation?*

7. Tell me about a business risk that you took that did not turn out as well as you had hoped and expected.

8. Tell me about a time you had a chance to take a risk, but decided that the risk was too high.

9. Tell me about a time you took a risk and failed.

10. Walk me through the riskiest work-related decision you have had to make in the last couple of years. *What factors did you take into consideration in making the decision? Were there any factors that you overlooked? How did the situation turn out?*

11. Describe a time when there was something you were working on that had a level of risk and tell me what you did to mitigate the risk.

12. Give me an example of a time when you enhanced awareness around safety, identified a risky process or procedure, etc.

Safety in the Workplace

1. In many situations, employees are required to wear protective equipment and may find it uncomfortable, cumbersome, or inconvenient to wear. Tell me about a time when this was true for you. (*NOTE: Make sure you find out what the equipment was, why the person did or didn't wear the equipment, and the factors that contributed to the decision.*)

2. Safety is not a one-person job. Give me an example of a time when you were able to improve safety only because you chose to involve others in making the improvement.

3. Tell me about the most challenging safety issue you have had to deal with. *What, specifically, made it challenging?*

4. Describe a time when you identified a potential safety issue and addressed it before a problem occurred.

5. Tell me about a way you have made your workplace a safer place for people to work.

Sales

1. We've all had customers who have threatened to leave us for one of our competitors. Tell me about a time when this happened to you and what you did to retain the business.

2. Tell me about your most difficult or demanding customers. *How were you able to work with them? Were you able to grow the business with them?*

3. Give me an example of a time you were able to anticipate a customer's complaint and take action before it became an issue.

4. Describe a time you were able to gain a client/customer through cold calling.

5. Tell me about a time your integrity was tested in a selling situation.

6. Tell me about a piece of business you lost where, in hindsight, there were actions you could have taken to prevent the loss.

7. Walk me through a time when, due to your ability to observe and listen, you were able to change tactics to turn a potential business loss into business retention or the sale of additional business.

8. Give me an example of a time when you were able to convince a skeptical or resistant customer to make the purchase. *How did you go about doing that? After the fact, did the customer feel that the purchase was the right decision? Why or why not?*

Self-Improvement, Learning, and Development

Positive Incidents

1. Tell me about a time when you had to learn something new or difficult in a short amount of time. *What created the situation? What did you have to learn? How did you learn it?*
2. Tell me about a time you had to do an unfamiliar task.
3. Give me an example of something that you have done in the past to improve yourself.
4. Give me an example of a situation when others knew more than you did. *How did you close the gap?*
5. Tell me about something specific you did to develop yourself that distinguished you from others.

Learning from Failure

6. Describe a time when you were not very satisfied or pleased with your performance. *What did you do about it? What did you learn? How have you applied that learning?*
7. Tell me about a time when you were able to treat a negative experience as a learning opportunity.
8. Tell me about a work-related decision you made or a situation you handled where, if you had it to do over again, you would do something different.
9. Describe a work situation that brought out the worst in you. *Why did it bring out the worst in you? What did you learn?*
10. Tell me about a time when one of your weaknesses got the better of you.
11. Tell me about a time you received constructive feedback from a boss or coworker that you took to heart and did something to correct.
12. We all have weaknesses that can interfere with our success. Tell me about one of yours and how you overcame it to be successful on a specific task or project.

(Use of) Social Media

1. Give me an example of a time when you used social media to enhance the image of your department or organization.
2. Tell me about a time when you needed to deal with negative comments or a brand reputation crisis on social media.
3. Give me an example of a time when your social media presence had a positive impact on your employer.

Failure

4. Tell me about a time when you missed a social media shift or innovation.
5. Describe what, to you, is your biggest social media failure. *Why do you consider it a failure? If you had it to do over again, what would you do differently? What did you learn from the situation? How have you applied what you learned?*

Stewardship/Corporate Citizenship

1. Tell me about a collaborative effort you headed (or were involved in) between your organization and the community.
2. Give me an example of how your understanding of a community issue helped you address a business problem, issue, or concern.
3. Describe for me something you were involved with in the community through which both the community and local businesses benefited.
4. Tell me about a way that you have championed the concept of corporate citizenship/stewardship within your team/department/organization.

Strategic Planning/Thinking

1. Tell me about a time when your industry knowledge alerted you to an upcoming challenge or opportunity and how you were able to develop a proactive strategy to deal with it.
2. Give me an example of a strategy you developed to achieve a long- or short-term business need, goal, or objective.
3. Give me an example of a time when, by using your understanding of the strengths and weaknesses of your competitors, you were able to gain a competitive advantage in the marketplace.
4. Tell me about a strategic initiative or opportunity you identified and pursued.
5. Give me an example of a time when you failed to align the strategic priorities of your department/team with the strategic priorities of the organization.
6. Tell me about a time when your ability to keep your eyes on the future proved to be a benefit to your organization/department/ team.

Stress Management

1. Tell me about a time when you were faced with stressors at work that tested your coping skills.
2. Give me an example of a time when you had to juggle a number of projects and priorities. *What were they? How did you manage to juggle them?*
3. Describe for me a time when your team was under a fair amount of stress. *What did you do to help them through this? Were you successful?*
4. Tell me about a time when you did not handle a stressful situation well.
5. Tell me about a time when a deadline was moved up on you and how you handled that. *Did you accomplish the task on time? How (or why not)?*

6. There are times we each feel overwhelmed with a task or project. Tell me about a time when this happened to you.

7. Describe a situation or time when someone or something really got under your skin.

8. Tell me about a project that required you to work well under pressure.

9. Describe one of the most stressful interactions you have had with an internal/external customer. *Why was it stressful? How did you handle it? How did the customer respond? In hindsight, how do you think you handled the situation?*

10. Tell me about a time when you were given an unrealistic, unreasonable, or unachievable goal or expectations. *Why do you feel it was unrealistic/unreasonable/unachievable? How did you handle it? How did it turn out in the end?*

Systems Management

1. Tell me about a time when your understanding of a social, organizational, or technological system helped you be more successful than you would have been otherwise.

2. Give me an example of a time when you picked up on a business or industry trend or change and made appropriate changes within your company/department/team to respond to or take advantage of the opportunity.

3. Describe a time when, had you been able to predict a business/industry occurrence, you would have been able to make adjustments so that your company/department/team did not suffer from it.

4. Tell me about a system you designed or improved. *Why did you do it? What benefit resulted? Who was impacted by the design/improvement? How did they react?*

Systems Thinking

1. Give me an example of a time when your ability to look at problems and issues from a big picture approach served you well.
2. Tell me about the most significant project you have worked on where it was crucial to keep track of details while still managing the big picture. *How did you make sure the work got done? How did you keep focused on the overall goal while still managing all of the specific parts?*
3. Tell me about a time when you failed to look at a problem or issue from a big picture perspective and paid the price for that.
4. Describe for me a time when your ability to find relationships between things inside and/or outside the organization made you more effective.
5. Give me an example of a time when you solved a problem in ways that addressed total system needs rather than just your immediate situation.

Taking Charge

1. Tell me about a time when you had to convince your team members to do something they didn't want to do.
2. Give me an example of when your staff reached a goal because they willingly followed your suggestions.
3. Give me a specific example of something you did that helped build enthusiasm for your staff.
4. Describe a time when you utilized your leadership ability to gain support for something that was initially strongly opposed by others.
5. Tell me about a time when you found it necessary to tactfully, but forcefully, say things that others did not want to hear.

6. Tell me about a time when you had to take charge and start the ball rolling to get a job done. *What were the ramifications if the job didn't get done?*

7. Describe for me the most unpopular stand you have taken in your job.

Teamwork (Encouraging and Building)

Getting Groups/Individuals to Cooperate

1. Provide an example of a time when it was critical that you establish an effective working relationship with an individual or group outside your department to complete an assignment or deliver a service.

2. Tell me about a time you needed to get two groups or people to work together effectively, who historically had never done so.

3. Give me an example of a time that your leadership transformed a group of people into an effective, healthy, productive team.

4. Tell me about a time you led a team that had one or more unproductive/negative members. *How did you find out about the unproductive member? What did you do? Why did you choose to do that? How did it work out?*

5. Give me an example of a time when you needed to get people who have very different work styles to work cooperatively on a project. *Were you successful? Why or why not?*

6. Describe a time when you had to have coworkers with different work styles or ideas work together on a project. *What, specifically, did you do to pull them together?*

Team/Team Member Strengths

7. Tell me about a time when you recognized a team member for having made a valuable contribution to the team.

8. Tell me about a time when, if it hadn't been for teamwork, your goal might not have been achieved.

Miscellaneous

9. Describe a time when you were able to build team spirit in an environment of low morale.

10. Tell me about a time when you needed to lead an intact or ad hoc team toward a goal that you, personally, did not completely support or believe in.

11. Give me an example of a time you successfully built a project team from scratch. *How did you go about selecting team members? How did you get these individuals to work as a team? What was the hardest part of getting them to work as a team? Was the team successful on the project?*

Failed/Negative Incidents

12. Give me an example of a time when you were less successful as a team leader than you would like to have been.

13. Tell me about a time when, because you didn't effectively build your team, you were not able to accomplish a task/project within specifications. *What did you learn? What would you do differently if you had it to do over again?*

Teamwork (Working as a Team Player)

Problems Among/with Fellow Team Members

1. Tell me about a time when you worked as a team member on a team that had one or more unproductive members. *What did you do? Why did you choose to do that? How did it work out?*

2. Give me an example of a time when others with whom you were working on a project disagreed with your idea.

3. Describe a time when one of the members on your team did not complete (or wasn't doing) her fair share of the work.

4. Tell me about a time when you helped others compromise for the good of the team. *What was your role? What steps did you take?*
5. Tell me about a time when you were part of a team that did not get along or did not work well together.
6. We've all been part of a work team or project team where there is one person who just rubs us the wrong way. Tell me about a time when this happened to you.
7. Give me an example of a time when you were willing to compromise on something relatively important to you so that your team could proceed with a project.
8. Tell me about a time when you were recognized and rewarded for being a valuable team member.

Failures/Disappointments

9. Give me an example of a time when you were not an effective team member.

Technology Management/Utilization

1. Give me an example of a time when you were responsible for selecting a new or improved technology.
2. Tell me about a time when you misinterpreted the intent or use of a piece of equipment.
3. Describe a time when you applied a new piece of technology to an existing task or project. *What benefits resulted from the technological application? How did you determine there would be a benefit?*
4. Give me an example of a time when you prevented, identified, or solved a problem with a piece of equipment.
5. Tell me about a time when you applied technology to improve a service, process, or productivity.

Time Management

1. Tell me about a time when you achieved a great deal in a short amount of time.
2. Give me an example of a time when you were unable to complete a project on schedule despite your best efforts.
3. Tell me about a time when you had to complete multiple tasks/ projects in a tight time frame.
4. Tell me about a time when you wasted an employee's time having them work on something that was unimportant to the organization but important to you.
5. Give me an example of a time that your priorities were changed quickly.
6. Give me an example to convince me that you can get more done in less time than others.
7. Give me an example of a time when you were effective at doing away with the constant emergencies and surprises in your department.

Trust

1. Tell me about a time when you mistrusted another employee, resulting in tension between the two of you. *What did you do to improve the relationship? Were you successful in improving it?*
2. Give me an example of a time when you failed to keep your boss informed of your actions or progress on a task or project.
3. Give me an example of a time that you failed to walk the talk at work.
4. Tell me about a time when you had to give the benefit of the doubt to someone at work.
5. Tell me about a time when your trustworthiness was challenged. *How did you react/respond?*

6. Tell me how you have developed trust and loyalty between you and your direct reports.

7. Describe a situation where you distrusted a coworker/supervisor, resulting in tension between you. *What steps did you take to improve the relationship?*

8. Trust requires personal accountability. Tell me about a time when you chose to trust someone.

Understanding Others

1. Give me an example to convince me that you understand why groups do what they do.

2. Tell me about a time you had to motivate a group of people.

3. Describe a time when your ability to pick up on the intentions or needs of a group resulted in you changing your course of action.

4. Tell me about a time when your understanding of what a group valued helped you work effectively with them.

5. Give me an example of a time when you were able to foresee a team's inappropriate course of action and help steer them in the right direction.

6. Tell me about a time when you gave someone or a group what they needed even though they didn't yet know it was needed.

Vision and Purpose

1. Tell me about a time when your vision of the future was so inspiring that you were able to convert naysayers into followers.

2. Tell me about a time when you lost track of the vision, mission, or purpose of your team/department/organization and it turned out to have repercussions.

3. Describe a time when you established a vision for your department/unit. *What process was used? Were others involved in setting the vision and, if so, how? How did the vision contribute to the functioning of the department/unit?*
4. Tell me about your goals in your current position and their relationship to the organization as a whole.
5. Tell me about a time when you anticipated the future and made changes to meet these future needs. *Did the anticipated future occur?*

5

FOLLOW-UP QUESTIONS

SOMETIMES, CANDIDATES WILL not provide complete STAR (Situation, Task, Action, Results) responses to a question; other times, you may simply want to get more information or clarification beyond what the candidate provided. There are a number of reasons that candidates don't give complete STAR responses. For example, candidates may be:

- Unfamiliar and therefore uncomfortable with behavioral/ competency interviewing
- Trying to avoid an area or issue
- In the habit of speaking in generalities
- Reluctant to talk for some specific reason
- Inherently shy

Whatever the reason, asking probing or follow-up questions allows you to get sufficient information on each situation to enable you to make an accurate assessment of the candidate's competency level. Probing questions are beneficial in at least four different ways: They provide real -world focus, gather and clarify information, uncover inconsistencies, and reveal additional competencies.

Real-World Focus

Probing questions enable you to focus the candidate on providing real-world examples. Since many candidates are not familiar with CBBI and may not be comfortable answering CBBI questions, they tend to fall back on comfortable behaviors: answering the question as if you posed a situational question (e.g., "What would you do if . . .") or answering with generic examples. Probing questions can be used to prompt the candidate to provide you with a specific example. The conversation, in this situation, may sound something like the following:

Interviewer: "We've all had to deal with unhappy customers from time to time. Tell me how you handled your most difficult customer."

Candidate: "The process I find to be the most successful in dealing with difficult customers is to first . . ."

Interviewer: "How often would you say you have to use this process?"

Candidate: "Probably about once a week."

Interviewer: "Tell me about the most difficult customer you've dealt with in the last couple of months."

Candidate: "Well, that would have to be the call I got from . . ."

Gathering and Clarifying

Probing questions provide a means for gathering additional information or clarification on the situation the candidate related. We have all personally been in the situation where we are telling a story to friends and we forget some of the details or assume that the people who are listening know certain things. The same thing happens during interviews. Candidates are nervous and will sometimes forget to provide some details. As a result, the story that you are hearing sounds incomplete or doesn't make sense. Follow-up questions help fill in the gaps in the story. For example, "You mentioned someone named Ashley. How does this person fit into the situation?"

Uncover Inconsistencies

When you are concerned about the authenticity of a candidate's story, probing questions provide a method for uncovering any inconsistencies. Probing or follow-up questions will test for consistency and inconsistency. They help you determine whether the candidate actually exhibited the desired behavior in that particular situation. For example, a candidate may relate a story in answer to a question and constantly say something like:

"First, we . . ."

"When we found out, we . . ."

"So we had to make adjustments . . ."

"Our goal at that point was to . . ."

These kinds of phrases should raise a red flag: Exactly who is "we"? The candidate could be using "we" for a number of reasons, including wanting to:

- Show modesty by not taking credit
- Convey that it truly was a team effort and everyone contributed equally
- Make it sound like he had a larger role than he actually did
- Take credit for something that others on the team actually did

The question you might want to ask, then, could be something like, "You said 'the first step we took when we discovered the discrepancy was . . .' Who, exactly, was 'we'?"

Discover Additional Competencies

Probing questions enable you to uncover nice to have competencies. Sometimes a candidate will make a comment while relating a situation that you would like to explore further. While it may only be indirectly related to the competency question, it could reveal that the candidate has *nice to have* competencies that could put her ahead of others, all else being equal.

Imagine that Position Y has a competency of *leading teams*. When responding to the behavioral question on this point, the candidate mentions a diversity issue. You work in an organization that highly values diversity—and has a very diverse workforce. Your probing question may be something like, "You said that when you were put in charge of that project team, there were some underlying tensions that you thought might be related to the diversity of the group. Tell me more about how you came to that conclusion and what you did."

Whatever your reason for using probing questions, remember that they need to be legal, nonthreatening, and nonjudgmental. They should only be used as a tool to uncover all the information you need to make a solid, valid assessment of the candidate's competency level.

Examples of Probing Questions

Some probing or follow-up questions are:

- Who did _____?
- Specifically, what did you do (or what was your role)?
- What did you say?
- What steps/actions did you take?
- I'm not sure I understand about _____ . Would you tell me more about it?
- You said _____ . I'm not sure I understand exactly what you mean. Could you expand on that some more?
- What happened after that?
- What were your specific duties or responsibilities?
- What was your specific contribution to the task or project?
- What did you say?
- How did the other person respond?
- How did the other person react?

- How did you react?
- How did you feel when _____?
- What was your role?
- What did you actually do?
- What did you actually say?
- What was the result?
- Who else was involved?
- What other options did you consider?
- What happened after _____?
- Why did you decide to do that?
- What was your logic/reasoning in doing _____?
- Tell me more about your interaction with (that person).
- What happened before _____?
- How did you deal with _____? (Followed by: Was that effective?)
- You said _____. Tell me more about that.
- Exactly how were you able to _____?
- What did you think when that happened?
- What were you thinking when _____?
- How did you deal with that?
- How did you know there was a problem?
- Why did that happen?
- How do you think other people felt about what you did?
- How did everything turn out in the end?
- What was the end result?
- What did you learn from the situation that you've described?
- Is there anything else I should know about that situation?
- Were you happy/satisfied with that outcome? Why (or why not)?
- What do you wish you had done differently?
- What did you learn from that?
- What were the obstacles you faced and how did you overcome them?
- What were you thinking at that point?
- How did you prepare for that?
- Can you be more specific about _____?

- Can you give me an example of that?
- What was going through your mind when you
  _____?
- If you could do it over again, what would you do differently and why?

There are a couple of things to keep in mind when asking probing questions. First, don't ask questions where the answer is obvious (otherwise known as "duh" questions). For example, "I imagine your next step in the process would be X. Am I right?" I can guarantee you that you are going to be right about 99 percent of the time. It's the rare applicant who will say, "No, my next step would be Z."

Second, avoid probing questions that could mislead, trick, or otherwise trap the applicant. This would include giving the impression you would do something that you wouldn't. For example, "I sometimes wonder if the only way to deal with a screaming customer is to just hang up on them. Do you think a customer who screams at you is a customer whom you really want to work that hard to maintain?"

Finally, it never hurts to remind ourselves that we should never ask a probing question—or any other type of question—that could be considered discriminatory, for legal as well as ethical reasons. Also do not, under any circumstance, ask questions that are not completely job-related.

6

GUIDELINES FOR INITIAL TELEPHONE SCREENING INTERVIEWS

WHILE IT MAY not be necessary to conduct an initial telephone screening interview for every position, telephone screening interviews are relatively commonplace because they are extremely cost- and time-effective. They help determine whether a candidate possesses the basic qualifications for the position—beyond those that appear on the résumé. These basic qualifications might include a specific experience or knowledge base (such as dealing with the federal government), a willingness to travel extensively, salary requirements, and other "must haves," or bona fide occupational qualifications (BFOQs).

In short, the telephone screening interview decreases the likelihood that you will bring candidates in for face-to-face interviews who look good on paper but don't have the basic requirements for the position.

An initial telephone screening interview may be applicable when:

1. There are basic technical skills required for the position that tend not to be readily apparent on résumés.
2. There are specific and essential abilities/capabilities that the candidate must possess, such as the ability to lift fifty pounds eight to ten times a day.
3. You are concerned that candidates may be looking for a higher salary than what the position pays.

4. There are specific position requirements that the candidate must be amenable to, such as a willingness to relocate or to travel a certain percentage of the time.

5. There is a need to learn more about the candidate's experience/ skills/knowledge beyond those listed on the résumé, without which he would not be a viable candidate.

If you decide that an initial telephone screening interview would be of value, you need to approach it with the same forethought and consideration as you would a face-to-face interview. Remember that you are representing the company when you conduct the screening interview and that the same legal guidelines apply as in a face-to-face interview. This would include calling the candidate in advance to schedule a mutually convenient time and date for the interview. You might also let the candidate know, at that point, that you will be conducting a CBBI telephone screening interview. The advantage of doing this is that the candidate is more likely to research CBBI and be prepared to answer these types of questions.

In addition to these considerations, there are five rules to conducting a successful telephone screening interview:

1. Develop and use a telephone screening interview form.
2. Keep the interview short.
3. Don't hold an in-depth discussion of the job requirements during the interview.
4. Conduct a legal interview.
5. Use the proper equipment.

Let's look at each of these individually.

Developing and Using a Telephone Screening Form

There is no magic number of questions to ask during a telephone screening interview, nor is there a required form (other than what your organization might require). While you can use a generic one-form-fits-all-positions telephone screening form, it will probably not serve you well. For example, I would hope that the basic requirements that would get a computer programmer's foot in the door for an interview would be different from those that would justify a face-to-face interview with a brain surgeon.

For a specific position, however, you should use the same form with every candidate you contact for a telephone screening interview. This ensures not only that you get the same information from all potential candidates—and that you get all the information you need—but that you do it in a legally appropriate and consistent manner.

The best approach is to come up with a position-specific telephone interview form. The good news is that once you develop the form, you will not have to redo it again until the basic requirements for the position change. Then it is simply a matter of making any necessary adjustments on the form, rather than rebuilding from scratch.

To determine what needs to be on the telephone screening interview form, start with your job description. Well-written job descriptions generally have the technical and special skills listed on them. If your job descriptions don't, you may need to start the entire hiring process with a job analysis. In either case, to ensure that you have all the critical bases covered on the telephone screening interview form, you may want to use a simple fill-in-the-blank process. For example:

> Candidates who do not have (specific knowledge/skill/experience/competency) do not meet the basic requirements for the position and, therefore, are not to be considered as potential candidates for the position.

Once you get the list done, you will find that some of the things you have listed can be readily found on any candidate's résumé (e.g., board certification, licensing). You would not, therefore, include these on the telephone screening interview form because the person should not even have made the cut to this point if these requirements were not found on the résumé. Once these obvious criteria are removed, the remaining criteria can then be used to develop the telephone interview screening form. While some of these questions may be behavior based, the primary focus of the telephone screening interview is to ascertain whether the candidate has the special/basic skills and technical background that would justify bringing her in for a face-to-face interview.

For some positions, there is a high technical component; for others, there is a high interpersonal skills component. To better look at how this mix might fall out, we can look at the mix of prequalifying factors on a matrix of interpersonal to technical skills, as shown in Figure 6-1.

Now, let's look at how this matrix might play out from three different quadrants. In the lower-right quadrant, one would find jobs that have a high interpersonal component with relatively low-level technical skill expertise required. The wide range of positions one might expect to find in this quadrant includes customer service representative, administrative assistant, sales consultant, receptionist, or cashier.

Let's look more in-depth at the sales consultant position, which is shown as (1) in Figure 6-1. This particular position is in a consulting organization that brokers a wide range of consulting services (e.g., organizational development, soft skills training, computer training, quality). In this organization, the job is highly "touchy-feely," requiring that the person in the position be able to read between the lines for needs, appropriately diagnose developmental needs, match needs with services, and build a solid working relationship with the client. In order to do this, the sales

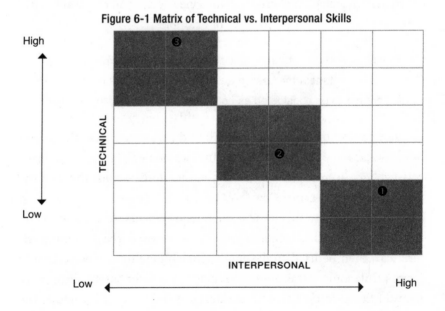

Figure 6-1 Matrix of Technical vs. Interpersonal Skills

consultant needs to have a basic understanding of the services being sold and know which would meet the client's needs. The sales consultant is not, however, required to be competent to perform any of the services she is selling. It is, therefore, quite low on technical skills requirements.

Some of the basic requirements for the sales consultant are experience in a wide range of industries, experience selling outside the company, ability to sell intangibles (services versus products), a consultative sales approach, demonstrated relationship-building skills, and effective communication and listening skills. These things are likely not readily apparent on a potential candidate's résumé. Since they are basic requirements, though, it would make sense to ensure that any candidate brought in for a face-to-face interview meets them. If you look at the Sample Telephone Screening Interview Form for sales consultants (Figure 6-2), you can see that these basic requirements can be found in the document.

You will also find, at the end of the form, a section for "other notes/comments." This section can be used to record additional, appropriate information you gathered from the candidate. For example, if in the course of answering a question, the candidate provided information indicating proficiency on a competency that is part of the interview process, the reference to that competency can be recorded in this section. A second use of this section is to record any relevant questions or comments from the candidate. For example, if he asks about the next step in the interview process and tells you that he'll be on vacation the following week, you could record "not available for interview week of_____."

Going back to Figure 6-1, the center quadrant would contain positions that have some technical requirements and that also require a moderate level of interpersonal skills. The absence of either would, in most situations, eliminate the candidate from consideration. Positions in this quadrant would likely include HR benefits administrator, bank loan officer, realtor, office manager, accounting manager, as well as some product sales personnel.

Let's look at the accounting manager in more detail, shown as (2) in Figure 6-1. In this particular organization, there are some technical aspects to the job of accounting manager that a candidate would have to know, or it would not be productive to pursue an interview. This would include technical/special skills such as:

Figure 6-2 Sample Telephone Screening Interview Form—Sales Consultant

	EXCELLENT	ACCEPTABLE	UNACCEPTABLE
Candidate's Name _____ Date _____ Interviewer _____			
What industries have you worked in? What percentage of time have you worked in each?			
What was your role in the sales organization? (Note: e.g., support, retail, inside, external)			
How would you approach a sales call with training or organizational development as your product or service?			
How do you go about building a relationship with a new client/customer?			
Which communication skill do you think is most important and why?			
Give me an example where your ability to listen effectively and ask good questions helped you exceed a client's/customer's expectations.			
❏ Recommend face-to-face interview with candidate ❏ Recommend not pursuing candidate			
Other notes/comments:			

- Bachelor's degree in accounting
- Skills in Excel, Access, and Word
- Experience in preparing and analyzing financial statements
- P&L background
- Experience with ADP Enterprise or PeopleSoft Payroll
- Financial and accounting report-writing skills
- Previous supervisory experience of a staff of at least six employees

Since some of these requirements (e.g., BS degree in accounting or payroll package experience) would be found on the résumé, they would not be incorporated into the telephone screening interview. Likewise, you may decide not to include any technical or special skills on which you would be willing to train the person. The remaining technical and special skills, then, would be used on the telephone screening interview.

In order for a person to be successful in a position in any organization there are also a number of interpersonal or soft skills that are required. For the accounting manager position in this example, there are four critical soft skills, without which the company would not be interested in pursuing a face-to-face interview. These include:

1. Experience and comfort with interacting effectively with top management
2. Ability to prioritize in order to meet deadlines
3. Written communication skills
4. Ethics/values/integrity

Putting this information into a telephone screening interview format, one might come up with something similar to the example for the accounting manager, as shown in Figure 6-3.

Figure 6-3 Sample Telephone Screening Interview Form—Accounting Manager

	EXCELLENT	ACCEPTABLE	UNACCEPTABLE
Candidate's Name _____ Date _____ Interviewer _____			
Give me an example of a complex financial statement you have prepared. What made it complex?			
Tell me about the most challenging experience you have had in the past couple of years writing a financial or accounting report. What made it particularly challenging?			
What was the largest number of direct reports you have ever had? In what functional areas? How did you handle the different personalities?			

	EXCELLENT	ACCEPTABLE	UNACCEPTABLE
Candidate's Name _____ Date _____ Interviewer _____			
Give me an example of a time when your attention to detail helped you avoid making a mistake or preserved the department's credibility.			
Give me an example of a time when, despite being tense or nervous, you were able to make a successful presentation to a higher-level management group.			
Tell me about a time you had a lot of tasks on your plate all at once. How do you decide what tasks to do and when to do them? Were there any deadlines you missed? If so, how did you handle the missed deadlines?			
Give me an example of an important report you have written. What made it so important?			
Tell me about a time you saw someone at work stretch or bend a rule, policy, or procedure beyond what you felt was acceptable. What did you do? Why did you take that action?			
❏ Recommend face-to-face interview with candidate ❏ Recommend not pursuing candidate			
Other notes/comments: 			

In the upper-left quadrant of Figure 6-1, one would find the more highly technical positions that require a relatively low level of interpersonal skills to be successful. One would probably find positions such as chemist, CAD operator, electrical engineer, or environmental technician in this quadrant. This is not to say that having good interpersonal skills might not be a hiring advantage for any of these positions (all else being equal). It simply means that one can be successful in these kinds of positions without being the belle of the ball.

Let's take a look at what a telephone screening interview format might look like for an environmental technician, shown as (3) in Figure 6-1. Unless the candidate possesses technical skills and/or knowledge such as the following, he would not be successful in that position in this particular organization:

- BS in biology, chemistry, toxicology, environmental science, or related field
- Experience with the state's regulatory requirements for risk assessment
- Experience with environmental site assessments
- HAZWOPER certification
- RCRA, CERCLA, NPDES knowledge
- Certificate for stack testing for air emission compliance
- Soil and surface water sampling and monitoring experience
- Data interpretation

What makes this job unique is a number of make-or-break job-related requirements that typically will not show up on any candidate's résumé. These include being able and willing to:

- Work in extremely hot or cold environments
- Periodically lift over twenty-five pounds
- Climb or crawl in confined spaces
- Work at heights in excess of four feet
- Wear a hazardous atmosphere respirator
- Work on call

When the interpersonal skills for success are examined for this position, we find far fewer than with the other two positions. The interpersonal skills include:

- Contractor relations
- Conflict management
- Written and oral communication skills

Putting this information onto a telephone screening interview form for this company (recognizing that it may not be the same requirements for every company with this position), the end result could look like the example for the environmental technician, as shown in Figure 6-4.

Depending on the position, there are many other factors that may need to be included in a telephone screening interview, such as being:

- Able and willing to work the hours required for the position (e.g., third shift, swing shift, an off-shift start-and-stop time)
- Able and willing to work overtime and/or weekends
- Willing to use her personal automobile for work-related travel
- Able to type within a specified typing range (e.g., 50–60 WPM)
- Able to operate a specific piece of equipment
- Fluent in another language
- Certified—if not already indicated on the résumé (e.g., certified Internet webmaster, SPHR/PHR, Microsoft-certified system engineer)

Figure 6-4 Sample Telephone Screening Interview Form—Environmental Technician

	EXCELLENT	ACCEPTABLE	UNACCEPTABLE
Candidate's Name _____ Date _____ Interviewer _____			
Tell me about the most difficult conflict you have ever had to solve with a contractor.			
Sometimes there are different interpretations of the sample data between the state, industry, and public sector. Give me an example of a time you experienced this situation. How was the situation resolved?			
Give me an example of a project you contracted out which had a large scope of work.			
Sometimes a contractor will shortcut specs. Tell me about a time when this happened to you. What did you do? What was the outcome?			

	EXCELLENT	ACCEPTABLE	UNACCEPTABLE
Candidate's Name _____ Date _____ Interviewer _____			
Please give me an overview of the kinds of memos, forms, permits, and reports you have had to write.			
What job-related training have you received outside of your degree?			

There are a number of working conditions that are required for the position. As I read through them, please let me know if you are able and willing—with or without reasonable accommodations—to work under the condition I describe:	ABLE/WILLING?	
	Yes	No
a. Extreme heat/cold environments		
b. Climb/crawl in confined spaces		
c. Work at heights in excess of 4 feet		
d. Periodically lifting over 25 pounds		
e. Wear a hazardous atmosphere respirator		
f. Work on call		

❑ Recommend face-to-face interview with candidate
❑ Recommend not pursuing candidate

Other notes/comments:

When conducting a telephone interview, regardless of the basic, essential job knowledge/skills you are screening for on the form, you would take notes relative to the potential candidate's answers. You would then check off the appropriate rating box or rate the candidate using another method. After the telephone screening interview, you would recommend whether to pursue a face-to-face interview with the candidate, that is, whether the candidate possesses the basic job requirements to warrant further consideration.

Throughout this chapter, the assumption has been that the telephone screening interview is conducted one-on-one. There are organizations that have taken other approaches. The most common alternate approach is to have a second person listen in or participate in the telephone screening interview. This person would also rate the candidate. The two interviewers would then compare notes and make a joint recommendation on whether to pursue a candidate. Organizations that have used this approach tend to report that the cost of having two people conducting the telephone screening interview is outweighed by the minimization of rater error.

Before we move off the first of the five rules to conducting a successful telephone screening interview, here is a warning on basic job requirements: Sometimes it is tempting to establish high requirements to attract the best candidates for the position. Be careful to establish the requirements in a nondiscriminatory manner. If you are uncertain as to the legality or appropriateness of a specific requirement, contact your legal department.

Keeping the Interview Short

A telephone screening interview is an opportunity to make sure that the potential candidate meets the basic needs for the position. As such, it should not be a full-blown interview. Generally, a telephone screening interview should be short and concise—typically no more than thirty minutes. Remember that your only purpose in conducting a telephone screening interview is to determine whether the potential candidate meets the basic requirements, without which it would not be of value to do a face-to-face interview.

Avoiding an In-Depth Discussion of the Job Requirements

At no point during the telephone screening interview should you discuss the specific responsibilities or required competencies of the position with the potential candidate. This information should be withheld until after you have gathered all of the data you want or need on the candidate, which would place this kind of disclosure toward the end of the first face-to-face interview. If information about the position is provided to the candidate too early, it is possible that she could answer even CBBI questions in a manner that would enable her to appear to be a stronger fit for the position than she actually is.

Conducting a Legal Interview

The telephone screening interview is part of the entire interview process; therefore, it must be legally conducted. Your documentation must be of the same appropriate nature as a face-to-face interview. Bottom line: Don't do or say anything that would be illegal in a face-to-face interview because the same rules apply. It is important to remember that when any telephone screening interview form is used, it is an interview document and it is treated as such. Specifically, all of the notes on the document must be job-related. If you are uncertain about any aspect of your interviewing process or form, meet with your legal department to review your concerns.

Using the Proper Equipment

Avoid conducting the telephone screening interview over a cell phone whenever possible. Before you object, it is recognized that many people only have a cell phone, and having a conversation on a landline is difficult if not impossible. Recognize, though, that cellular reception can have a significant impact on the screening interview. A friend of mine who was a candidate for a director-level position suffered through a telephone screening interview conducted over a recruiter's cell phone. The reception was so poor that he could only hear about half of what the recruiter was saying, and he kept having to ask the recruiter to repeat or clarify what she was asking. After a few minutes, my friend suggested that the interview be rescheduled for another time, and the recruiter said, "That's okay. I can hear you just fine." The moral of the story: It is important not only that you be able to clearly hear and understand the candidate, but that the candidate be able to clearly hear and understand you. When you couple this problem with the dropped signals that can also plague cell phone interviews, you can end up with a telephone screening interview that has been so disrupted that it is practically worthless.

By the way, my friend was offered the director position mentioned above, but declined. While not the deciding factor, the cell phone interview did play a part in his decision.

CREATING AN INTERVIEW GUIDE

E VERY ORGANIZATION DESIGNS its own interview form or guide, one that works most effectively with its culture and the needs of its interviewers. Regardless of the final form the document takes, a well-designed interview guide will have at least three sections:

1. Summary/overview
2. CBBI questions
3. Rating scales

This chapter examines each of the three sections of an interview guide and provides sample formats for each.

Summary/Overview

The summary/overview is a one- to two-page quick reference of all the critical information on the candidate (see Figure 7-1). While to some this section may seem to be additional, unnecessary paperwork, it can actually save time when you get to the point of comparing the ratings of one candidate to another. When all this information is clearly and neatly contained at the beginning of the interview document, there is no need to fumble through the pages of the document looking for specific ratings or notations.

As shown in Figure 7-1, the technical and special skills of the position are noted first. The logic in doing this is that this is one of the first items you review on a candidate's application to determine whether to proceed with an interview. In this example, there are two different rating scales used within the Technical and Special Skills section. The first applies to requirements that are either/or, as in "either you have it or you don't." For example, the candidate either meets the job requirement of having a bachelor's degree in chemical engineering or he doesn't meet that requirement. There are no shades of gray.

Figure 7-1 Interview Form for [Position]: Summary/Overview

Candidate _____
Interview Date _____
Interviewer _____

TECHNICAL AND SPECIAL SKILLS		
(e.g., preferred degree)	Rating Scale	❑ 5 Possesses ❑ 0 Does Not Possess
(e.g., certification)		
(e.g., license)		
(e.g., quality experience such as Six Sigma)	Rating Scale	❑ 0 Does Not Possess ❑ 1–2 Minimal ❑ 3–4 Average/Adequate ❑ 5–6 Above Average ❑ 7–8 Excellent
(e.g., specific technical knowledge such as a specific world-class manufacturing technique)		
(e.g., experience such as number of years in a specific industry)		

COMPETENCIES	
Competency and Definition	Rating

STRENGTHS	WEAKNESSES

OTHER COMMENTS

Recommendation

❑ Recommend to hire (with satisfactory background and reference check)

❑ Continue to interview—strong candidate

❑ Continue to interview—need to resolve issue(s) around _____

_____

❑ Recommend not hiring _____

❑ Other (specify) _____

This kind of rating makes sense for degrees, licenses, certifications, and similar requirements. The second rating scale applies to requirements in which there is a range of acceptable fit. In the example in Figure 7-1, an eight-point Likert scale is used, with two points per descriptor. Any point distribution—from a three-point to a ten-point scale—is acceptable as long as it is easily understood by those who will be using the scale.

Figure 7-2 Strengths and Weaknesses: Good vs. Poor Examples

POOR EXAMPLE	
STRENGTHS	WEAKNESSES
+ fast-paced	Micromanage?
GOOD EXAMPLE	
STRENGTHS	WEAKNESSES
High tolerance for working in a fast-paced, stressful environment. See answers to Ambiguity #2, Flexibility #1.	The company the candidate currently works for is—in his words—tightly managed. Examples provided indicate that the company may micromanage its employees. (Competency A, #1: "Even if we know the right thing to do, management tells us to do something different." Competency C, #2: "Yes, I did ask why we were doing X instead of Y. I was to just do it; my job wasn't to ask questions," and "Following directions—explicitly—is simply the best course of action." Because of these comments, I'm concerned about his ability to function effectively in this loosely managed company.

The next component of the summary/overview is the competencies section. Each competency is defined according to how the company is using that term or phrase. The rating the interviewer gave the candidate on the applicable competency is also recorded on the form. Note that because not all interviewers will be assigned questions on every competency, there are likely to be some competencies for which an individual interviewer will not be rating a candidate.

The third component of the summary/overview is the most subjective part of the interview process. In this section, the interviewer has an opportunity to record impressions of the candidate's strengths and weaknesses, as well as other observations. It is strongly suggested, though, that each of these subjective observations be tied as closely as possible to answers the candidate provided in response to specific interview questions.

Figure 7-2 shows two very different recordings of strengths and weaknesses. The shorthand entries in the "Poor Example" could create a problem for the interviewer and when at a later review she may not remember what she was referring to when she originally made the notations. Does

"+ fast paced" mean that the person works well in a fast-paced environment or that he is looking for a fast-paced work environment? Does "micromanage?" mean that the person is a micromanager or that the person was micromanaged? The more time that has passed since the interviewer wrote these cryptic notes, the less likely it is that she will be able to explain them completely and accurately.

The "Good Example," on the other hand, provides sufficient detail to jog the interviewer's memory, enabling her to fully discuss the candidate.

CBBI Questions

The CBBI questions are the second section found in the interview guide. These are the pages that contain the CBBI competencies and questions. It is recommended that there be one page for each competency, allowing sufficient room for the interviewer to make appropriate interview notes.

It is not required, but it is strongly recommended that the STAR process be incorporated into the CBBI questions section. Because CBBI focuses on real-world experience, it is important to get all the facts relevant to the situation the candidate is presenting. The STAR process, as illustrated in Figure 7-3, guides the interviewer to do this.

Figure 7-3 The STAR Process

Situation	What was the situation the candidate was faced with or what did he or she need to accomplish? What were the circumstances?
Task	What tasks did the person accomplish to deal with the situation? You may need to ask probing questions on the Task and Action to ensure that you are finding out what the candidate did, especially if the candidate talks about what "we" did.
Action	What specifically did the candidate do to accomplish the task? (NOTE: Make sure you know what the *candidate's* actions were. Some people will use phrases such as "We did . . ." or "We discovered . . ." when they didn't do anything themselves. When you hear "we" statements, make sure you follow up and clarify. (See the Probing/Follow-Up Questions chapter for more information.)
Results	What was the outcome? Were the tasks accomplished? Did the actions solve the situation with which the candidate was faced? What did the candidate learn from the experience?

Another consideration in developing each CBBI questions page has to do with whether the rating scale is on the same page as the competency and questions or whether it is separate. Figures 7-4 and 7-5 illustrate CBBI questions pages that are set up without the rating scale. This is, of course, not the only setup option available. The best setup is the one that works for the interviewers. Regardless of the format you choose to use, there should be one page for each competency. Figure 7-6 will give you a better feel for what this page might look like as part of an interview packet.

Figure 7-4 Competency Format Example A

Candidate _____	
Interview Date _____	
COMPETENCY: [listed and defined with desired behaviors]	
Behavioral interview question #1 Behavioral interview question #2 (if appropriate/applicable)	
Situation **T**ask **A**ction **R**esults	#1
Situation **T**ask **A**ction **R**esults	#2

Figure 7-5 Competency Format Example B

| Candidate _____ |
| Interview Date _____ |

COMPETENCY: [listed and defined with desired behaviors]

(Behavioral interview question #1)

Situation   **T**ask   **A**ction   **R**esults

(Behavioral interview question #2)

Situation   **T**ask   **A**ction   **R**esults

Figure 7-6 Example Page from Interview Packet

Candidate: Jane Doe

Interview Date: 5/8/XX

COMPETENCY: CUSTOMER FOCUS

Listens to and works to understand the customer (both internal and external), anticipating customer needs and focusing on customer satisfaction.

- Dedicated to meeting the expectations and requirements of internal and external customers.
- Gets firsthand customer information and uses it to improve products and services.
- Acts with customers in mind.
- Creates and maintains effective relationships with customers.
- Has the trust and respect of customers.

1. Tell me about a time when you did your best to resolve a customer or client concern and the individual was still not satisfied.

Situation   Task   Action   Results

2. Give me an example of a time when you had to handle an angry customer. (Recommended follow-up question: How would you assess your role in defusing the situation?)

Situation   Task   Action   Results

Rating Scales

The third and final section in a well-designed interview guide is the rating scale. There are two primary options for rating scales. One is developing a form where the rating scale is part of the CBBI questions page. The second primary option is to have a separate document for the rating scales. This can either be a completely separate document or a page following the CBBI interview questions.

In addition to the organization's culture, the biggest factor in determining how to incorporate the rating scale is the design of the rating scales, which are often referred to as *behaviorally anchored ratings scales* (BARS) or *behavioral observation scales* (BOS).

Rating scales can range from very simple scales that apply universally to all competencies to very complex and detailed scales that apply to each specific competency. In their purest sense, a BARS or BOS will reduce rater discrepancies by linking a numerical rating with specific and defined behaviors at various points along the rating scale.

The more detailed and structured the BARS or BOS, the greater the consistency tends to be across raters on the same competency for the same candidate. That is, if two people interview a single candidate on a single competency, the more clearly defined the scale, the more likely the interviewers are to agree on the rating for the candidate. The drawback to this specificity is, however, that developing this kind of competency -by-competency detail can be very frustrating, arduous, and time -consuming. With that said, it must be remembered that this is a one-time effort. Once the time has been put in to develop a specific rating scale for a competency, the rating scale would apply to every position with that competency across the organization.

That does not mean that the specific competency rating scale is always the best choice. What is best will depend upon the organization's culture, practices, and overall approach to interviewing. Let's look at this range of options, starting with the most basic rating scale.

Basic One-Scale-Fits-All-Competencies Rating Scale

The scale in Figure 7-7 is an example of a very basic rating scale that one could apply to all competencies. While the example uses a 6-point Likert scale, any numbered Likert scale could be used (e.g., 1 to 4 or 0 to 10). The scale could either be incorporated in each page of the interview guide or it could be placed in the summary/overview section.

Figure 7-7 Basic Rating Scale: 6-Point Likert

0	1–2	3–4	5–6
Does not meet basic requirement	Meets the basic requirement	Slightly exceeds the basic requirement	Significantly exceeds the basic requirement

A universally applied rating scale is quick and easy to develop and use. However, it can lead to significant rating disagreements between raters. For example, let's say that we are interviewing a candidate on the competency *effective listening skills*. I may believe that anyone who has the patience to sit and listen to another human being for more than five seconds without fiddling with something on their desk and who periodically makes eye contact with the speaker is demonstrating outstanding listening skills. You, on the other hand (being a highly trained, skilled, and talented manager), believe that active listening means that the person maintains eye contact, uses paraphrasing to check for understanding, asks questions to gain a better understanding, and uses nonverbals effectively and appropriately. If we used the scale in Figure 7-7, it is highly likely that the two of us would rate any given candidate very differently. When it comes to discussing the candidate, we would be likely to have a very active conversation about where the candidate should really be rated on the *listening* competency.

Figure 7-8 More Detailed One-Size-Fits-All Rating Scale

RATING		DESCRIPTION
−1	Negative	The situation described as a positive example was inconsistent with the company's definition of proficient performance of this competency. OR When relating a negative example, either no learning occurred from the situation or the learning was inconsistent with the company's definition of proficient performance of this competency.
0	Absent	The candidate was unable to provide an example.
1	Somewhat Effective	The candidate demonstrated most of the indicators for successful performance in this competency; the example was relatively acceptable; candidate could, with coaching/development, meet the competency as defined.
2	Proficient	The candidate successfully demonstrated the competency as defined by the company; the candidate's example indicates an ability to successfully employ the knowledge/skills/abilities required to effectively perform this competency.
3	Excellent	The candidate described handling this situation in a manner that exceeds expectations; the described behavior went beyond the company's definition for proficient performance in concrete measurable or observable ways.
4	Leader	The example provided by the candidate indicates that he or she would be considered a role model for others. He/she would be able to lead, train, and motivate others to be excellent in the competency.

If we bump the scale up a bit, we can still look at a one-size-fits-all-competencies approach, but one that will give interviewers slightly more direction. Figure 7-8 (using a −1 to 4 scale) and Figure 7-9 (using a 0 to 8 scale) show more detailed approaches.

Figure 7-9 More Detailed 8-Point Likert Rating Scale

RATING	DESCRIPTION
7–8 Far Exceeds	• Described behavior far exceeds all reasonable expectations. • Behavior is of a rare high quality, found only in a small percentage of people in organizations. • Clearly recognized as being consistently distinguished in skills, behavior, knowledge, understanding and/or usage. • Demonstrates a very high degree of expertise. • Would serve as a model of excellence or as a coach to others. • The candidate's proficiency on this competency compares with the best this company has seen.
5–6 Exceeds	• The candidate's described performance clearly and consistently exceeds that of a fully proficient person. • The candidate's answer indicates that performance is above the expected level in fulfilling the competency for this position. • The candidate demonstrated noteworthy proficiency in handling the described situation.
3–4 Proficient	• The candidate described performance/behavior/skill utilization consistent with that of an individual whose performance is solid, consistent, and dependable in this proficiency. • The related incident indicates the candidate understands and applies the criteria for success in demonstrating this competency.
1–2 Needs to Improve	• The candidate's description of the application of the competency is slightly below the standards acceptable for this organization. • Information was provided by the candidate that indicates learning and development have occurred from the incident, but the competency is not yet to company standards.
0 Not Acceptable	• The candidate was unable to provide an acceptable example of the utilization of the competency. OR • The example provided by the candidate fell substantially short of the expected level of performance on the competency. • The candidate did not indicate any learning from the situation and/or felt that the performance/behavior/skill demonstrated was acceptable.

Rating Scale Keyed to Each Competency

To get any more specific, one has to move into a competency-by-competency rating scale. Figure 7-10 provides a sample fill-in-the-blank format that could be customized for each competency. These rating scales would then either be incorporated into the interview form or provided as a separate document for the interviewer.

Figure 7-10 Competency-Specific Fill-in-the-Blank Rating Scale

COMPETENCY:		Rating:	
Definition:			
–1	Negative	Evidence gathered indicates candidate's ability to _____ is severely lacking.	
0	Absent	The candidate was unable to provide an example of his/her ability to _____.	
1–2	Somewhat Effective	The candidate made a few minor missteps and is, therefore, less than proficient; however, he/she recognized his/her errors, took corrective action, and learned from his/her mistakes; development has occurred and the candidate's potential for continued development is evident.	
3–4	Proficient	• •	• •
5–6	Excellent/ Leader	• Is a role model for others • Mentors others	•
Reason for Rating:			

The most significant disadvantage to incorporating individual competency rating scales into the interview packet is that it could result in the interviewer carrying a good-sized—and intimidating—tome into the interview. On the other hand, keeping these rating scales as separate documents means that the interviewer could make assumptions about how each rating level reads without referring to the actual wording of the rating, resulting in rating errors. A happy medium might be to remove the rating space from the interview document and provide the interviewer with two separate documents: an interview form and a rating form.

An example of how this might look when it is completed for the *staff development* competency is shown in Figure 7-11.

Figure 7-11 Staff Development Competency Rating Scale

COMPETENCY: STAFF DEVELOPMENT	Rating:	
Definition: Fosters the short- and long-term growth and development of direct reports through OJT, mentoring, coaching, classroom, online, and other appropriate avenues.		
−1 Negative	Evidence gathered indicates candidate's ability to grow and develop his/her staff is severely lacking; evidence supplied by the candidate indicates either clearly inappropriate development measures were employed, or the results were negative in some other manner.	
0 Absent	The candidate was unable to provide an example of his/her ability to develop employees.	
1–2 Somewhat Effective	The candidate made a few minor missteps and is, therefore, less than proficient; however, he/she recognized his/her errors, took corrective action, and learned from his/her mistakes; development has occurred and the candidate's potential for continued development is evident.	
3–4 Proficient	• Believes that employee development is a critical part of his/her job • Provides constructive feedback (not criticism) • Knows the career goals of each of his/her direct reports • Designs and executes, with employee input, a developmental plan for each employee	• Holds developmental review and planning meetings twice a year with each employee • Is able to determine the most appropriate method for staff development, with or without input from the OD department • Has a track record of providing direct reports with opportunities for growth within their positions as well as outside their positions

5–6	• Is a role model for others	• Will hire, or accept in transfer, an employee who has potential, but needs some coaching/mentoring
Excellent/ Leader	• Mentors others	
	• Holds at least quarterly developmental review and planning meetings with each employee	

Specific Examples to Explain Rating:

Competency and Rating Layout

As mentioned earlier, there are two primary choices on how to lay out the interview form in terms of the CBBI questions and the rating scale: combined or separate. To help you determine which might be the best choice for your organization, Figures 7-12 to 7-17 present examples of different layouts.

Combined competency and rating layout examples can be found for the competencies *giving/receiving information* (Figure 7-12) and *values diversity* (Figure 7-13). Separate competency and rating sheets can be found for the competencies *ethics and integrity* (Figures 7-14 and 7-15) and *results oriented* (Figures 7-16 and 7-17).

Figure 7-12 Giving/Receiving Information Competency and Rating Layout

COMPETENCY & DEFINITION:				
Giving/Receiving Information—Maintains open lines of communication up, down, and across the organization, as well as inside and outside the organization.				
BEHAVIORS				
● Obtains input from others as and when appropriate	?	–	✓	+
● Expresses opinions, views, and ideas in nonthreatening manner	?	–	✓	+
● Ensures that the opinions, values, and ideas of others are heard	?	–	✓	+
● Provides timely updates	?	–	✓	+
● Ensures people have the necessary information to work effectively	?	–	✓	+
● Uses the appropriate communication vehicle	?	–	✓	+

Q1: Tell me about a situation where, because you had a strong network, you were able to gather information that others were not able to secure.

Q2: Describe a situation where you delayed providing someone with information that would have been valuable to them.

NOTES: S T A R

Competency Rating: ❏ 4 - Leader ❏ 3 - Exceeded ❏ 2 - Met
❏ 1 - Nearly Met ❏ 0 - Not Demonstrated

Figure 7-13 Values Diversity Competency and Rating Layout

COMPETENCY: VALUES DIVERSITY	Rating:
Unacceptable (0)	<ul><li>Doesn't deal well with people different from self</li><li>Uncomfortable with differences between people</li><li>Doesn't see business value of diversity</li><li>Stereotypes people/groups</li></ul>
Proficient (3)	<ul><li>Handles diversity issues in timely and appropriate manner</li><li>Hires for talent and potential without regard to race, nationality, culture, disability, and/or gender</li><li>Conforms to and supports all company policies, procedures, and guidelines on diversity</li></ul>
Exceptional (6)	<ul><li>Proficient plus:</li><li>Proactive in addressing diversity</li><li>Actively seeks out and recruits a diverse workforce</li><li>Models inclusive behavior</li><li>Actively seeks out opportunities to work with individuals different from self</li><li>Coaches others on diversity issues</li></ul>
Q1: Tell me about a time when you adapted your style in order to work effectively with those who were different from you.	Q2: Tell me about a time when you took action to make someone feel comfortable in an environment where people were obviously uncomfortable with his or her presence.
NOTES:	NOTES:

Figure 7-14 Ethics and Integrity Competency

COMPETENCY:
Ethics and Integrity—Relies on a solid set of core values to provide guidance through good and bad times; behaves in ways that engender trust and respect.
Tell me about a specific time when you had to handle a tough problem which challenged fairness or ethical issues.
Situation   Task   Action   Results
NOTES:
Tell me about a time when you saw someone at work stretch or bend a rule, policy, or procedure beyond what you felt was acceptable.
Situation   Task   Action   Results
NOTES:

Figure 7-15 Ethics and Integrity Rating Form

ETHICS AND INTEGRITY	
Relies on a solid set of core values to provide guidance through good and bad times; behaves in ways that engender trust and respect.	
Behavioral Standards	• Adheres to company's code of ethics and integrity • Keeps promises • Maintains confidentiality • Admits mistakes • Provides honest, helpful feedback • Does not overlook inappropriate or marginally inappropriate behavior in others; handles in an effective, timely manner • Exemplifies the highest standards of honesty, integrity, and ethical business behavior • Practices what he/she preaches • Holds self and others accountable for acting with integrity and being ethical
RATING	
❏ Example demonstrated most, if not all, of the above behavioral descriptors (as marked). The candidate would be an excellent ethics and integrity coach/leader/mentor.	Rating Explanation
❏ Example demonstrated the majority of the above behavioral descriptors, as marked.	
❏ Example demonstrated compliance with only a few of the above behavioral descriptors.	
❏ Example provided was unethical or failed to meet the above behavioral descriptors.	

Figure 7-16 Results-Oriented Competency

RESULTS ORIENTED:
Focuses on achieving—or exceeding—goals; has a propensity toward action and accomplishment.
#1: Tell me about a time when you were asked to complete a difficult assignment and the odds were against you. What did you learn from the experience? #2: (optional) Tell me about a time where you did not achieve the results you should have or in the time frame you should have.

Situation Task Action Results	#1
Situation Task Action Results	#2

Figure 7-17 Results-Oriented Rating Form

RESULTS ORIENTED
Behaviors:

❏	Demonstrated strong personal sense of purpose
❏	Set/accepted challenging goal
❏	Focused on getting the desired/expected results
❏	Conveyed an appropriate sense of urgency for the situation
❏	Persisted/persevered in the face of obstacles and roadblocks
❏	Didn't procrastinate; brought closure to the task/project within agreed upon time frame
❏	Maintained a high level of productivity
❏	Focused on the critical few rather than the trivial many
❏	Demonstrated high personal standards of achievement (standards of excellence)
❏	Monitored own progress and provided updates to appropriate person(s)
❏	Demonstrated a willingness to make the personal sacrifices necessary to be successful

NOTES:

Rating		
Exceptional	6	7
Proficient	4	5
Marginal	2	3
Unacceptable	0	1

Regardless of the rating scale used, there should be some place on the form (preferably near the rating scale) for the interviewer to make notes relative to why he rated the candidate at a specific level. Let's assume that the notes the interviewer made for the *composure* competency are as follows:

Gave a good example. Lots of experience. No problem answering follow-up questions. Obviously got this one down!

What's the primary problem with this? Even if there is only one day—and a couple of interviews—between writing this comment and meeting to make the final hiring decision, chances are that the interviewer will not be able to remember what the "good example" was and what it was that indicated that the candidate has "got this one down."

As part of their training, all interviewers should be taught how to write specific, effective, job-related rating notes. For example:

Presentation to board. Not all charts had been updated by staff—forgot to check (accepted responsibility). Didn't know some information a board member asked—got "ripped apart" (deep breathing, listening). Handled department-related questions outside of material being presented (using appropriate humor—e.g., question on future of department). Volunteered what was learned from this situation (planning, checking work, practicing presentation, anticipating related/unrelated questions) and how to incorporate learning into future presentations.

Notes like this record the specific details of the situation and provide reminders as to why the interviewer rated the candidate at a particular level. Even if there are events occurring between the interviews and the discussion of the candidates, with such detailed notes the interviewer is more likely to be able to remember the specifics of the candidate's situation and to fully discuss why he was rated at a particular level.

8

SMART WAYS TO ASSEMBLE THE DATA FROM MULTIPLE INTERVIEWERS

Too often when there are multiple interviewers, everyone has their own form, their own perspective as to which competencies are most critical, their own way of asking questions, and their own way of rating performance. Then, when the interviewers sit down to discuss each candidate, it becomes a lot like the process of comparing apples and oranges.

This chapter presents two forms that will help increase the chances that you are comparing apples to apples. The first form, the Individual Candidate Rating Form (Figure 8-1), combines the ratings of all of the interviewers for a single candidate.

Figure 8-1 Individual Candidate Rating Sample Form

INDIVIDUAL CANDIDATE RATING FORM			
Candidate Name	Position:		
1. SKILLS & COMPETENCIES	**2. INTERVIEWERS' INITIALS**		**3. AVERAGE**
	Rating		
Technical & Special Skills			
Competencies			

The information for the Skills and Competencies column (1) comes off of the first page of the interview sheet. This is simply a cut-and-paste process.

In the middle section (2), the interviewers' initials are recorded along with their individual ratings for those skills or competencies they covered during their interview. In most situations, not all interviewers will ask questions on all the skills or competencies for a position. Where multiple interviewer ratings are available, they are averaged for each skill and each competency, and the average for each is recorded in the Average column (3).

Once an Individual Candidate Rating Form has been completed on each candidate, a cumulative report—the Comparison of Candidates Form (Figure 8-2)—is assembled, enabling a side-by-side quantitative comparison of the candidates.

Once again, the information for the Skills and Competencies column (1) comes off of the first page of the interview sheet. At the top of the right columns, the name of each candidate is recorded (2). Finally, the average rating for each candidate's skills and competencies is copied off each Individual Candidate Rating Form and recorded in the appropriate columns (3).

Once the information is assembled on this form, a discussion can be held about each of the candidates. It can then be decided who should be offered the position, pending any background check, reference check, or other organizational hiring requirements.

Figure 8-2 Comparison of Candidates—Sample Form

1. SKILLS & COMPETENCIES	2. CANDIDATES' NAMES			
	3. AVERAGE RATING			
Technical & Special Skills				
Competencies				

9

USE THE COMPETENCIES IN YOUR OTHER PROGRAMS AND PROCESSES

Now that you have established competencies and are hiring candidates against them, it makes sense to start incorporating the competencies into your other human resource programs and processes. In this chapter, we will briefly look at some of the next competency-integration steps you could take.

Performance Management

One of the many reasons employees dislike annual performance reviews is that they feel the review is arbitrary and capricious. They may view it as something that is being done to them that really has little importance or value rather than view it as a tool that can be used to help them improve in their position and grow with the organization.

Competencies can help change that mindset. When individual performance is linked to business performance, the organization's performance management process begins to take on value in the organization. Employees start to see the link between their day-to-day work activities and the organization achieving its mission, vision, and strategic plan—as well as operating in accordance with its values and ethics statements. Besides, it only makes sense that if you are going to hire people according to competencies that you also evaluate their performance against those same competencies.

What the actual performance management forms look like may well differ for nonexempt and exempt employees. Let's look at the basic requirements for each.

Nonexempt Employees

It is recommended that, at a minimum, the form for nonexempt employees contain these five sections:

1. **Competencies with BARS and Rating Scales.** In most organizations, this section is significantly more straightforward than what one would find with an exempt position. Figure 9-1 illustrates a competency with rating, excerpted from a nonexempt performance review.

2. **Accomplishments/Achievements.** Even though ongoing feedback is an integral part of effective performance management, too often we forget to tell our direct reports about the good

Figure 9-1 Competency with Rating—Excerpt from Nonexempt Performance Review

QUALITY OF WORK	
Consider the ability to produce accurate work that meets company standards.	
Far Exceeds	Very few errors. Consistently does high quality work. Data accuracy is high. Is a role model and/or coach for others.
Exceeds	Seldom makes errors. Work is usually correct with few errors and is of good quality. Data accuracy is good.
Meets	Quality is above minimum standards. Occasionally makes errors but seldom repeats after correction. Data accuracy is acceptable.
Needs Improvement	Work often needs regular inspection. Makes more errors than should.
Unacceptable	Makes excessive and repetitive mistakes. Cannot be given work requiring accuracy.

things that they have accomplished during the year. This section is a reminder to either point these things out or summarize the positive feedback you have given the employee during the course of the year.

3. **Areas for Improvement.** This section details what needs to be improved, how it needs to be improved, and by when.

4. **Summary/Overall.** This section contains any summary comments you wish to make, a place for the employee to comment, as well as an overall performance rating. An example of what this might look like for an hourly position is shown in Figure 9-2.

5. **Sign-Offs.** This section is where appropriate signatures and dates are recorded.

Exempt Employees

Figure 9-2 Performance Summary for an Hourly Position

OVERALL PERFORMANCE SUMMARY AND RATING		
Supervisor Comments:		
Employee Comments:		
	Far Exceeds	Outstanding overall performance. Employee consistently performs job-related tasks at high levels of competency. Is a role model and/or coach for others.
	Exceeds	High level of achievement. Employee clearly demonstrates the ability to excel in job-related tasks.
	Meets	Acceptable level of performance. Employee generally meets the expectations.
	Needs Improvement	Minimum level of performance. There are a number of areas in which improvement is needed.
	Unacceptable	Unsatisfactory level of performance. Significant improvement in many areas must be demonstrated quickly.

For exempt employees, it is recommended that sections such as the following three also be included:

1. **Individual Goals.** These goals should be set using the familiar SMART format, which is that goals should be Specific, Measurable, Achievable, Realistic, and Time-Bound.

2. **Summary/Overall.** As with the nonexempt form, this section is the place for the leader and employee to make overall comments.

3. **Learning/Development Plan.** This section includes any goal or performance factor on which the employee did not meet expectations, any additional learning/development she needs to meet current or future expectations in her present position, and any learning/development required for a position into which she may be moved or promoted within the next eighteen months. It would NOT include a development plan for performance problems or succession planning.

Regardless of what the actual exempt form looks like, integrating competencies into your company's performance management process ensures that performance is being measured against the competencies that have been determined to be critical for success in the position and/or the organization. An example of how this might look on an actual form is illustrated in Figure 9-3.

Figure 9-3 Competencies Integrated into Exempt Performance Review For

DEVELOPS EMPLOYEES.	
Provides challenges/stretching tasks/assignments. Holds frequent development discussions. Is aware of direct reports' career goals. Constructs and executes compelling development plans. Pushes direct reports to accept developmental moves. Accepts direct reports who need improvement/development. Is a people builder. Completes timely performance reviews.	❏ Far Exceeds ❏ Exceeds ❏ Solid Performance ❏ Needs Improvement ❏ Unacceptable
Rationale for rating if other than "Solid Performance":	
PLANNING, ORGANIZING, AND SETTING PRIORITIES.	
Accurately scopes out projects. Sets SMART goals and objectives. Breaks work into bite-sized process steps. Develops clear, specific schedules and people/ task assignments. Anticipates and adjusts for problems. Measures performance against goals. Brings together appropriate resources to get things done. Uses resources effectively and efficiently. Spends own time and time of others on critical few and puts trivial many aside. Eliminates roadblocks. Creates focus.	❏ Far Exceeds ❏ Exceeds ❏ Solid Performance ❏ Needs Improvement ❏ Unacceptable
Rationale for rating if other than "Solid Performance":	

Incorporating competencies into the performance management process is a first step in getting everyone in the organization to understand that they play an important part in the organization's overall success. This in turn leads to benefits including:

- Improved business results
- Motivated employees
- Higher morale
- Increased productivity
- A strong, solid base of high-performing employees

Individual Performance Improvement Plans

When an employee's performance does not meet expectations, development plans can be created—either through the performance management process or as a separate document. Such plans identify the development that needs to occur and the competency to which the development relates. In general, the more specific each item on the development plan is—particularly in respect to what acceptable performance looks like—the more likely it is that the person will be able to model the competency at the required level.

Learning and Development

Learning and development curriculums or individual programs can be developed and provided—instructor-led or through e-learning—to ensure that employees have the skills necessary to demonstrate the competency to the required level. An example of a progressive skill level training and development opportunity is shown in Figure 9-4.

Figure 9-4 Sample Progressive Skill Level Learning/Development Opportunity

	LEARNING/DEVELOPMENT OPPORTUNITY FOR *HIRING/STAFFING* COMPETENCY
Level 1	Attend an approved CBBI program.
Level 2	Work with a recruiter to develop your skills. Process: 1. Observe the recruiter during at least two interviews; debrief each afterward. 2. Co-interview at least three candidates with recruiter; debrief each afterward. 3. Interview at least three candidates while the recruiter observes; debrief each afterward.
Level 3	Participate as an interviewer during two campus recruiting sessions. Follow-up debrief with recruiter(s) who attended each session.

Succession Planning

Succession planning used to be easy. The CEO decided who would be slotted into what position based on hunches, instincts, intuition, and, quite often, politics. Today, if it is done well, succession planning isn't that easy. Having a succession plan—and consistently monitoring, modifying, and updating it—is probably one of the most important and challenging components of building an organization that is capable of achieving its strategic plan and goals.

To be effective and valued, succession planning must be a formal, ongoing, systematic, and dynamic effort that ensures that the right people, with the right skills, are in the right place at the right time and ready to assume a new leadership position in the organization. When succession planning is done against the organization's competency model(s), future leaders are assessed, selected, and developed with the future of the organization in mind.

Competencies blend in well with virtually any approach that a company takes for succession planning. When competency-based succession planning is done well, the process is:

- Aligned with the business strategy and its goals and objectives
- Supported by the organization's culture, vision, mission, and values
- Integrated with other HR processes

The bottom line is that when competency-based HR systems are developed and used consistently throughout the organization, they link employees to the company's tactical and strategic direction. This consistency sends a strong message throughout the organization as to what is required for individual and organizational success. The end result, then, is that individuals and organizations not only survive but thrive in today's competitive environment.

10

CBBI ADVICE FOR JOB SEEKERS

THE FIRST EDITION of my book was written with the hiring manager and human resources in mind. After publication, though, I received feedback from job seekers who commented that the book was overly slanted toward hiring managers and didn't give them as much information to prepare for the interview as they would have liked. While both the first and the second editions are, intentionally, focused on helping human resources, recruiters, and hiring managers ask questions that will help them select the best-fit person for the position, I recognize that job seekers don't always have a solid understanding of what CBBI is about. This chapter is designed to provide an overview of the CBBI process to help candidates more confidently approach behavioral-based interviews. Recognize, though, that there is no "how to answer the question" material here. This is because everyone's past experience is different and what different interviewers are specifically looking for in their CBBI questions may be different.

Why Are You Being Asked CBBIs?

Competency-based behavioral interview questions are designed to determine if you have the competencies (skills, behaviors, aptitudes) that lead to success in the position for which you are interviewing. They are based on the premise that how you have acted in situations in the past is likely the way you will behave in those same or similar situations in the future. They are asking you, in essence, to tell a factual story of a time when you were in a specific kind of situation. For example, they may be interested in your competence around conflict management and ask you about a time that you had a conflict with a coworker. The assumption is that if you handled a conflict with a coworker effectively last week, you are likely to handle any future coworker conflict in that same—or a similarly effective—manner.

CBBI questions help interviewers better gauge your fit for the position and the organization. They also help interviewers identify where there might be skill gaps, so they can determine whether it is a skill gap they are willing and able to help you close or it is too large or difficult to close.

For example, imagine the interviewer asked you to describe the most difficult customer you've ever had to deal with. Also pretend that the company has been able to write a description of the kind of difficult customer they have and, on a 10-point scale, their difficult customer is an 8. When you describe your situation, the interviewer looks at the scale and says that you're describing a level 6 difficult customer. That's within the acceptable range for the company to be willing to help you close that skill gap.

On the other hand, the interviewer might ask a question about acting with integrity/being ethical. For example, you might be asked, "Give me an example of a time when it would have been easier to tell a white lie than the truth" or "Describe a time someone at work asked you to reveal confidential information." In its interview guide, the company has defined what behaviors it expects to see as a 10 on a 10-point scale. If your story only meets its definition of a 4 on the scale, the interviewer may choose to pass on you as a candidate because it's hard to help someone learn how to act with integrity or to be more ethical.

Prepare for the Interview

You're not going to be handed a list of CBBI questions prior to the interview, so how do you prepare? You will find plenty of information on the Internet for behavioral interview questions. Be careful, though, of those sites that say "Here are the top 5 behavioral interview questions you need to be prepared to answer" or "Ace the interview with these answers to the top 10 behavioral interview questions." It's just not that easy. While it is true that some of these questions may show up in the interview, the exact phrasing and focus is going to depend on the company and job you are applying for. Additionally, these websites cannot give you the answers to the stories of your life and work experience.

So you are going to have to put in the hard work. Start by making two lists. For the first list, think about your career from a broad perspective and the experiences—good and bad—that you have had. Questions you might want to ask yourself—and jot down brief answers to—include:

- What are the biggest business/career successes I have had?
- What are the biggest failures I have had and what did I learn from them?
- What are some of the most significant business challenges that I have had to tackle?
- Where have I excelled?
- What stories would my boss tell about my work accomplishments/failures?
- What stories would my coworkers tell about my work accomplishments/failures?
- What stories would my direct reports tell about me (from a business/team member/leadership perspective)?

For your second list, look at the job description or advertisement for the job, and identify what the company lists as the competencies. Identify the behaviors, expectations, and interpersonal skills that the position requires rather than technical skills. For example, if you are looking at a project manager position, you may see something similar to the following in a job ad:

. . . looking for three years' experience working with high-performance, collaborative teams. Must be flexible and able to deal tactfully and diplomatically with others. Strong verbal and written communication are critical as is exceptional attention to detail . . .

In this part of the advertisement, there are a number of competencies identified: high-performance, team collaboration, flexibility, tact and diplomacy, strong verbal/written skills, and attention to detail.

This second list, then, gives you some possible competencies around which you are likely to be asked behavioral questions. Your first list will (hopefully) provide you with some examples of ways you have demonstrated these competencies.

For example, if we look at the advertisement, it says that one of the competencies the project manager needs is to be *flexible*. Look through the first list that you created, and try to find a situation that demonstrates you being flexible (e.g., a time that you were halfway through Project X when Y changed in the organization and made it necessary for you/your team to make a major change to Project X). In some situations, you may not have anything on your original list that you believe demonstrates flexibility. That doesn't mean that you've never demonstrated that competency. It just means that you need to think a little more to come up with an example.

After you connect the dots between the competencies for the position and your experience, come up with a compelling and succinct summary of the experience. This story should last less than two minutes. The easiest way to organize your story is by using the STAR approach:

- Situation—Give a brief description of the situation or event. This is designed to provide a context or background for the remainder of your story. You should highlight the key information to give an overview and set the stage.
- Task—This explains specifically what you were charged with doing or what tasks you were responsible for in the situation or event. If the story you are telling is about a team effort, focus on what you did, not what the team did. For example, "On the team, my primary role was _____."
- Action—Describe the actions that you took, highlighting any challenges or constraints you experienced. Avoid using "we" because all the interviewer is interested in are the actions that you took during the situation or event.
- Results—Summarize the outcomes of the situation or event. If

there was a quantitative outcome, make sure you mention that. It's much more impressive to hear, "As a result of the actions I took, there was an average 15-minute decrease in customer wait time" rather than "As a result, customers didn't have to wait as long, and that made them a lot more satisfied."

When you tell your story, be careful about the use of the word "we." Using "we" consistently during your story has a negative feeling associated with it for most interviewers. The impression may be that you are using "we" to take credit for something you had just a minor role in doing. You can, however, say something like "We had a change in senior leadership. As a team, we typically did X. As a result of the change, my contribution to X (what you used to do) had to change, and I had to do (what your new responsibility was). How I adapted to that was . . ."

There are an unlimited number of ways you can combine the individual components of STAR together to structure your answer in a smooth and succinct way. For example:

- "A good example is when (situation). I was responsible for (task). (Actions you took.) In the end, (result)."
- "As (an organization/a department/a team), we were experiencing _____ , so the decision was to _____ . My contribution was _____ and I (actions you took). It was the right thing to do because (results)."
- "Recently, when I was working on (task), I discovered (situation). Because of that, I (action). Because of this, (result)."

If you have a situation where there were complications or impediments, you might want to slightly embellish STAR by responding in ways such as these:

- "One situation that comes to mind is (situation). My role was (task), and I (action). There were a few complications along the way. One was (complication), and what I did was (action). The other was (complication), and I (action). Because these challenges were addressed, (result)."

- "One of my responsibilities is X (situation and task). Normally, doing that is straightforward but because of (a change/complication), my normal process wasn't going to work. To get my task completed correctly and on time, I (action). As a result, (result)."

Where many candidates run into challenges is when the example that comes to mind is a situation that did not turn out well or when the interviewer asks for a specific failure example, such as:

- Describe a time at work when you let something important fall through the cracks.
- Tell me about a time that you got upset or frustrated with someone at work.
- Give me an example of a time you were unsuccessful in getting your point across to someone at work.

Contrary to what you might be thinking and despite what many websites will tell you, these are not trick questions. The interviewer is not trying to find a way to eliminate you from the candidate pool, but you may be eliminated if you answer the question poorly or say that you've never experienced that negative situation. As human beings, we are all flawed, so the worst thing that you can do is to try to present yourself as perfect, never having experienced conflict with coworkers, never having discovered a mistake until it was too late, never wishing you had a "do over" button you could push. When you fail to provide those very human examples of failure, all you are going to do is tick the interviewer off and call into question your honesty and, potentially, your level of self-awareness.

When faced with these questions, focus on answering in a professional, diplomatic, and mature manner. Hopefully you learned from the situation, so that learning—and how you've applied it—should be part of your answer. Most interviewers are less concerned about the fact that you failed at something and more concerned that you recognized the failure, took appropriate action, learned from the situation, and applied your learning to the same or similar situations in the future.

If you were asked a question such as "Give me an example of a time you made a decision that later turned out not to be the best possible decision," your answer might be something like this:

"Situation A is a good example of that. I was responsible for (task) and did (action). Unfortunately, I made some decisions (provide examples) that resulted in (problem/complication/failure area). Once I discovered the mistake (or the mistake was brought to my attention), I (describe the action you took). I learned _____ from the experience. On a similar project a couple of months ago, I remembered Situation A and (describe how you used what you learned from the problem)."

Let's look at a slightly different question that could still be a negative example, even though the wording is positive. "Tell me about a situation in which you had to adjust to changes over which you had no control." Your answer might be:

"A recent example is my work on Project X. The initial plan was _____. I was responsible for _____. I had accomplished _____ when I found out (new information). As a result, some major changes needed to be made quickly in Project X, so I (what changes you made). As a result, (what the outcome was)."

Now that you've had some good examples of using STAR to answer a CBBI question, let's look at an example of how you do not want to respond to a behavioral interview question. I warned you earlier about blindly following advice on the Internet, and this is an example of why caution is warranted.

In one article that purported to provide the best answers to behavioral questions about a variety of topics, the author recommended the following response to a question about receiving criticism:

". . . We discussed the problem . . . and my boss learned that (the problem) . . . was not my fault . . . Another manager failed . . ."

Why is that a problem? Because, as the interviewer, I am going to expect that if you need information from someone for you to complete your work and you don't get it in a timely manner that you are going to follow up with that person. That story sounds to me like you failed to follow up, do the right thing, and take accountability. It says to me as the interviewer that you chose, instead, to blame the other manager for you not getting your work done. If I'm looking for someone who is responsible and accountable, you have one big strike against you.

Also, be cautious about adapting a suggested answer as your own. There are some candidates who think, "Well, that never happened to me, but it certainly could have. So I'm going to use that suggested answer if I get asked a question on that competency. I know enough about that kind of situation that I can fake it and make it sound like mine."

Adept interviewers will see right through that. It's really hard for you to convincingly tell a story that isn't yours. Skilled interviewers are going to ask follow-up and probing questions, they are going to ask you to be more specific about certain actions, they are going to request an explanation as to why you chose one path over another, they are going to expect you to explain how and why you made certain decisions, and so on. When you're using a fake or adopted story, you're not going to have those answers available, and a great interviewer is going to see the holes in your story. You're much better off telling a simple real-life story over adopting a made-up story that you can't be specific about. When those holes show up in your answers, you're branding yourself negatively and putting yourself out of running for the position.

Once you've identified some likely competencies and identified stories from your past that illustrate your skills, it's time to practice. Do it out loud for a few reasons. First, it gives you an opportunity to hear how your story sounds. Second, there are times when sentences or word combinations sound good in your head but not spoken out loud. Finally, the more comfortable you are in telling your story, the less likely you are to use filler words like *um, uh, like, right?* and other phrases. Make sure you time yourself as you do this, too, to ensure that your stories are two minutes or less, otherwise it may feel to the interviewer like you are rambling.

Practice in front of a mirror, seated as you would be in an interview. This gives you a chance to see yourself as the interviewer will see you. You'll be able to identify if you are making odd facial expressions that could be interpreted negatively. You can also check your gestures to make sure that they support your story, but aren't distracting.

Remember, you cannot prepare for a specific behavioral question, but what you can do is come up with solid, succinct examples that demonstrate your ability to successfully execute the competencies required for the position.

Finally, use words that you are comfortable with, that you can pronounce properly (e.g., it's *escape* not *exscape*; it's *anyway* not *anyways*; it's *supposedly* not *supposably*), that you know you are using properly (e.g., it's *more fun* rather than *funner*; it's *we were* not *we was*; you are *detail-oriented* not *detail-orientated*), and that are real words (e.g., *irregardless* is not a word, nor is *flustrated*). Your inability to properly use the English language (or what we allow to pass as English in America), will, for many interviewers, count against you—particularly if you are interviewing for a client/customer facing position. If you're not sure about the language you are using, ask someone who knows and can properly advise you.

During the Interview

Since you have taken time to think about specific situations throughout your career that demonstrate some of the potential competencies for the position, and you've practiced your answers to the questions so they are smooth, clear, and succinct, you are going to be well prepared for a behavioral interview—or at least as prepared as anyone can be for one. There are, however, three scenarios that you may face during the interview that you should be prepared for.

First, you may be asked a behavioral question to which a specific situation doesn't come to mind. In these situations, there is nothing wrong with saying, "Let me think a minute about a good example for you." An interviewer isn't going to expect you to instantly recall every single example of everything you've done throughout your entire career. You are not going to "lose points" by taking a minute to come up with a good example. (You will, however, make a bad impression by saying that you can't think of anything—particularly if you haven't taken a minute to try to come up with a situation.) Once you have a situation in mind, you can quickly formulate that example into a STAR response.

Second, you're going to interview with some people who are poor interviewers, though they may be armed with behavioral interview questions. In these situations, you may occasionally be asked a complex, confusing, or convoluted behavioral question, and you may not be sure exactly what the interviewer is asking. There are a couple of different approaches you can take. First, you could paraphrase what you think the interviewer is asking you. For example, "Let me make sure I'm providing the kind of example you want. Are you looking for an example of a time that I ____ ." If you're right, the person will say so and if you are not, they are likely going to ask you the question again, hopefully in a way that is easier to understand.

The other approach you can take is to simply ask for clarification. For example, if you truly can't even begin to guess what the person is asking you, simply say, "I'm not sure I understand what you're looking for. Could you ask me the question again in a slightly different way?" Typically, the person is going to paraphrase their question in a more straightforward manner.

Third, you may be asked a question where you honestly cannot come up with a real situation for the question the interviewer is asking. In this case, do not—under any circumstance—make up a story or use a story from a friend or coworker. You are likely to trip yourself up and appear to be dishonest, which will absolutely cost you the job. If you don't have a story of your own, you should simply own up to the fact. If you have a situation you've experienced that is similar, you might offer that up. For example, "I've never been in that exact situation; however, I was in a similar situation where I had to (related skill or competency). I'd be glad to share that situation with you if you'd like."

During the interview, you will likely be faced with follow-up questions from the interviewer. This is often done to probe more into your story to get details or clarify information to determine how close a match you are for what is needed in the position. You may be asked questions such as:

- What did you think when _____ happened?
- What was your reaction to _____ ?

- How did you feel when _____?
- Tell me more about _____ .
- You mentioned that "we" did _____ . What exactly were your responsibilities/actions?
- When you got to the decision point, why did you choose to pursue _____ instead of _____?
- Exactly how did you approach _____?
- What did you say or do when you encountered _____?
- What was the financial impact of that?

If you've told a story that is completely honest, you are going to have no problem answering these probing and clarification questions.

What if You're Not Asked CBBI Questions?

What if you've prepared to answer CBBI questions, but find that you're getting traditional questions? The temptation will be to feel relieved and fall back on your tried-and-true traditional responses to "What are your greatest strengths?" and "What are your greatest weaknesses?" and "Why should we hire you?" I strongly recommend that you resist the temptation and keep to your CBBI STAR answers.

For example, when you are asked, "What are your greatest weaknesses?" respond with a failure story that you learned from. For example:

"One weakness I have is _____ . When (situation), I was responsible for (task). I (actions you took). Unfortunately, that meant (failure). What I learned was _____ . The next time I was in that situation, I (how you applied your learning)."

After the Interview

A thank-you email after the interview is an absolute must. If you really want to make an impression, though, send hand-written notes customized to every person with whom you interviewed.

Hopefully you took notes during the interview, can recall some of the competencies the interviewer was looking for, or both. Use this as the basis to write your thank-you note. Let's say, for example, that you were asked the following questions:

- Tell me about a time when you did your best to resolve a customer or client concern, and the individual was still not satisfied.
- Describe a time when you came up with a creative solution to a work problem you had been dealing with for some time.
- Give me an example of a time when you had to adjust quickly to changes over which you had no control.

Within your thank-you note, you may want to say, ". . . I am confident that my ability to handle difficult customer situations, come up with creative solutions to problems, and work effectively in a changing environment will contribute to my success in the X position with ABC Company . . ."

We've all been through interviews in which, after leaving, we think of something relevant to the job that we forgot to mention. Again, use your thank-you note to add this information in addition to reinforcing the job fit information you shared during the interview.

While it isn't possible to prepare completely, using the information contained in this chapter will give you confidence going into the behavioral interview. The fact that you are able to provide STAR answers to questions will impress most interviewers. Writing a thank-you email or note will demonstrate a courtesy and politeness that others often forget. Will it get you the job? That part is up to your ability to showcase your skills as a match for the position and the organization. Good luck!

Resources and References

Interviewing, Competencies, Competency-Based Interviewing, and Behavior-Based Interviewing

There are, combined, literally thousands of books, white papers, journal articles, and Internet articles on these topics. Although each article has something to offer, it would be impossible to list all of the resources here. Following, though, are a few resources to help you enhance various aspects of your recruitment, interviewing, and hiring process.

Books

Adler, Lou. *Hire with Your Head: Using Performance-Based Hiring to Build Great Teams.* New York: John Wiley & Sons, 2007.

Arthur, Diane. *Recruiting, Interviewing, Selecting & Orienting New Employees.* New York: AMACOM, 2012.

Camp, Richard R., Mary E. Vielhaber, and Jack L. Simonetti. *Strategic Interviewing.* San Francisco: Jossey-Bass, 2001.

Cohen, David S. *The Talent Edge: A Behavioral Approach to Hiring, Developing, and Keeping Top Performers.* New York: John Wiley & Sons, 2009.

Falcone, Paul. *96 Great Interview Questions to Ask Before You Hire*, 2nd edition. New York: AMACOM, 2008.

Fear, Richard A. and Bob Chiron. *The Evaluation Interview: How to Probe Deeply, Get Candid Answers, and Predict the Performance of Job Candidates.* New York: McGraw-Hill, 2002.

Fry, Ron. *Ask the Right Questions, Hire the Best People*, 3rd edition. Franklin Lakes, N.J.: Career Press, 2010.

Murphy, Mark. *Hiring for Attitude: A Revolutionary Approach to Recruiting and Selecting People with Both Tremendous Skills and Superb Attitude.* New York: McGraw-Hill Education, 2011.

White Papers

"Competency-Based Interviews." An Intelligence Executive white paper from Armstrong Hall, 2012.

"Integrating HR & Talent Management Processes." Workitect, Inc., 2011.

Nemerov, Donald S. and Stephen Schoonover. "Competency-Based HR Applications Survey: Executive Summary of Results." Alexandria, Va.: Society for Human Resources Management White Paper, 2001.

Robert Tearle Consulting. "White Paper: Interviewing Framework." An Intelligence Executive white paper from Armstrong Hall, 2013.

Articles

While I cannot say I support this approach (and I can actually see a significant number of potential drawbacks), I also believe it is important to be aware of what is trending:

Sullivan, John. "Text-Interviewing—The Next Big Thing in Recruiting?" *ERE Media*, September 12, 2016. https://www.eremedia.com/ere/text-interviewing-the-next-big-thing-in-recruiting/.

The articles below on the behavior- and competency-based interviewing process will give you an idea about just how a wide variety of business journals publish information on the subject.

Bock, Laszlo. "Here's Google's Secret to Hiring the Best People," *Wired*, April 7, 2015.

Bradley, Elizabeth. "Hiring the Best," *Women in Business* 55.4, July/August 2003.

Kelly, Maura. "The New Job Interview," *Rolling Stone*, p. 67, March 15, 2001.

Knight, Rebecca. "How to Conduct an Effective Job Interview," *Harvard Business Review*, January 23, 2015.

Trotsky, Judith. "Oh, Will You Behave?" *Computerworld* 35.2, January 8, 2001.

Watterson, Thomas. "More Employers Using Job Interview as a Test of Applicants' Mettle," *Boston Globe*, Boston Works section, September 12, 2004. (Note: While the article is good, the questions at the end of the article are, for the most part, not behavior-based.)

Wright, Daisy. "Tell Stories, Get Hired," *Office Pro* 65.6, August/September 2004.

"Interview Questions That Hit the Mark," *Harvard Business Review* 6.3, March 2001.

Notes

Chapter 3

1. Mark Murphy, "Why New Hires Fail (Emotional Intelligence vs. Skills)," *Leadership IQ*, June 22, 2015.

2. Shawn Achor, "Positive Intelligence," *Harvard Business Review*, January-February 2012.

3. George Brandt, "Top Executive Recruiters Agree There Are Only Three True Job Interview Questions," Forbes.com, April 27, 2011.

4. Serena Ng, Susan Pulliam, and Gregory Zuckerman, "Buffett: Combs Is 'a 100% fit.'" *Wall Street Journal*, October 27, 2010.

5. Kristin Hoppe, "Justworks Has a Stellar Work Culture. Here's How We Hire to Keep It," Justblog, April 28, 2016.

6. "1 in 5 Employers Has Unknowingly Asked an Illegal Interview Question, Career-Builder Finds," CareerBuilder, April 9, 2015.

Index

accomplishment (competency), 91

accountability (competency), 64

accounting manager
 skills matrix, 140
 telephone screening interview form
 for, 143–144

action orientation (competency), 64–65

adaptability (competency), 88–89

adaptation, and diversity, 85

allocating resources (competency),
 114-115

ambiguity, ability to deal with
 (competency), 65

analytical skills (competency), 65–66

anticipation, and job skill, 90–91

approachability (competency), 66

assertiveness (competency), 66–67

attention to detail (competency), 82

bad decisions, 81

behaviorally anchored rating scales
 (BARS), 159

behavioral observation scales (BOS), 159

behavior/performance
 and culture fit, 44–45
 interviewing to assess, 17–18, 19–20
 in non-interview settings, 46–49

Bock, Laszlo, on brainteaser interview
 questions, 10

BOS (behavioral observation scales), 159

bottom line contribution (competency), 67

brainteaser interview questions, 10–13
 advantages of, 11–12
 examples of, 11
 lack of information from, 55–57
 problems with, 12–13

"Brainteaser or Interview Torture Tool?"
 (Peterson), 12

budget (competency), 67

Buffett, Warren, on culture fit, 43

building relationships (competency),
 67–68

business acumen (competency), 68

candidates, 185–196
 benefits of CBBI for, 34
 conduct during interview, 193–195
 interactions of, with employees, 47, 49
 interview follow-up, 196
 interview preparation, 186–193
 reasons for CBBI questions for,
 85–186
 responses to traditional interview
 questions by, 195

career ambition (competency), 68–69

caring about direct reports
 (competency), 69

CBBI, *see* competency-based behavioral
 interviewing

CBBI questions section, of interview
 guide, 155–158

cell phones, avoiding interview over,
 149–150

challenges, for goal setting/
 accomplishment/focus competency, 92

change, and flexibility, 89–90

change management (competency), 70

change-related initiative, 2, 96

Combs, Todd, 43

comfort around higher management
 (competency), 70–71

communication (competency), 71–72

Comparison of Candidates Form, 175

compassion (competency), 73

competency-based behavioral
 interviewing (CBBI), 15–35
 advantages of, 33–35
 candidate's understanding for use of,
 185–186
 converting to, 22–30
 defining, 16–18
 objections to, 30–33